21st Century Capitalism

Robert Heilbroner

21st

Century
Capitalism

W · W · NORTON & COMPANY

NEW YORK · LONDON

First published as a Norton paperback 1994

The text of this book is composed in Times Roman,
with the display set in Janson.
Composition and manufacturing by the Haddon Craftsmen, Inc.

Library of Congress Cataloging-in-Publication Data
Heilbroner, Robert L.
21st century capitalism / Robert Heilbroner.
p.   cm.
Includes index.
1. Capitalism—United States. 2. Twenty-first century.
I. Title.
HB501.H395   1993
330.12′2′0973—dc20   93-7662

ISBN 0-393-31228-3

W. W. Norton & Company, Inc., 500 Fifth Avenue, New York, N.Y. 10110
W. W. Norton & Company Ltd., 10 Coptic Street, London WC1A1PU

2 3 4 5 6 7 8 9 0

For Sammy,
when he gets a little older

Contents

Acknowledgments

THESE PAGES ARE based on the Massey Lectures that I was privileged to give in the fall of 1992. Hence my first thanks go to the Canadian Broadcasting Company and to Massey College for their invitation to speak on that distinguished series, and in particular to Bernie Lucht, the executive director of the Ideas program on which the lectures were carried. I am grateful as well to the House of Anansi Press which published the manuscript on which those lectures were based with exemplary speed and skill.

Since then, I have added additional material of a philosophical and historical kind that seemed ill-suited to a series of broadcast talks. That material was presented in a final lecture at Massey College, presided over by Ann Saddlemyer, Master of the College, whose warm support was deeply appreciated. The contents of that lecture, now incorporated into the Introduction and the last chapter, are themselves adaptations of an essay, "History's Lessons," published in the December 1992 issue of *Social Research*.

Acknowledgments

Finally, I thank my dear friend Peter L. Bernstein and my much esteemed colleague William Milberg for their warm criticisms, and Donald Lamm for his patience and guidance, and for being my editor and publisher for almost twenty years.

1
Introduction

"HISTORY TEACHES NOTHING, but only punishes for not learning its lessons." The bitter aphorism, from the late Russian medievalist Vassily Kliuchesky,[1] speaks directly to a generation that has lived through what must be the most instructive century in modern civilization but wonders whether it has grasped its message. History seems to be telling us that the gradient of human progress is imperceptible, perhaps even zero, so that there should be no occasion for dismay in discovering that a hundred years of courage, imagination, and sacrifice have brought us back to Square One. I recall a discussion I had ten years ago with an old friend, an eminent anthropologist, in which we reviewed the hatreds of Hindu and Muslim, Muslim and Jew, Jew and Arab, Irish Protestant and Catholic, white and black, tribe and tribe, and the passions aroused by women's rights. "And we thought this was going to be the century of enlightenment!" my friend had said. What would he

1. Quoted in Vladimir Smelev and Nikolai Popov, *The Turning Point,* New York, Doubleday, 1989, p. 75.

13

say today, in the light of the aftermath of communism, launched within our lifetimes as an attempt to rewrite the future of humankind; the reappearance of swastikas in Poland and skinheads in East Germany, both thumbing their noses at the "victory" of World War II; the carnage in Yugoslavia which says as much for World War I; and the spectacle of a triumphant capitalism in the present condition of the United States.

Kliuchesky's aphorism strikes directly at any effort to write about the prospects for the immense span of a century. It raises questions whose immensity is matched only by their elusiveness: What is left of the idea of progress in human affairs? Does some form of socialism still lie ahead, as the successor to capitalism? Is human nature at the root of our problems? These are questions I shall address in these pages, but only indirectly and glancingly, until the very end. This is because I believe they are best examined through a focusing lens that scales them down to graspable dimensions and poses them in imaginable contexts. That lens, as the title of this book already makes clear, is the outlook for the social order in which we will live during the coming century.

That is not quite so audacious an undertaking as it sounds. Twenty-first-century capitalism begins in less than a decade, so that at its nearest it is almost at hand. Thereafter it stretches into the future for a hundred years—a period that we can, however dimly, include within our present concerns, which we could not, were we asked to think about the prospects for capitalism—or, for that matter, for humanity—in the year 3099. Thus I use the term "century" to demarcate a future to which we can apply our faculties of reasoned and plausible discourse, from a more distant future to which the only applicable mode of consideration is that of piety or despair. And I use the word capitalism—largely American capitalism—because it focuses our attention on the great familiar *terra incognita* within which the twenty-first century will be played out for most of my readers. At any rate, here is where I shall seek not only for whatever clarification we may find with respect to the options and obstacles ahead in our own futures, but for clues as to the lessons that must be learned if humanity is to minimize—it will surely not escape—history's punishments.

2

Capitalism from a Distance

I

THE VERY TITLE *21st Century Capitalism*
sounds as if I were about to make predictions
on a grandiose scale, but to the relief or disappointment
of my readers, I must make clear that such is not my
intention. In the 1970s I once had occasion to discuss the
success of economists in foreseeing large-scale events
during the twenty-odd preceding years—events such as
the advent of the multinational corporation, the rise of
Japan as a major economic power, and the emergence of
inflation as a chronic problem of all industrial nations.
Not a single one of these world-shaking developments
had been foretold.[2] More recently, there have been a
number of equally important, world-scale happenings,
such as the decline in productivity suffered by all the
Western powers or the striking loss of global economic
leadership of the United States. How presciently were

2. Robert Heilbroner, "The Clouded Crystal Ball", *Papers and Proceedings,* American Economic Association, May 1974.

these developments anticipated by the great research institutions that carry on their continuous radar sweep of
trends? The answer is that none foresaw them. Finally,
there is perhaps the largest economic turning point of
modern history—the collapse of the Soviet economy. I
do not know of a single economic organization, including those privy to all the secrets of government intelli-
gence services, that expected the debacle.

So I will not be so foolish as to attempt to do that
which has foiled so many—namely, to predict the future
of the social order in which we live. How, then, can I
speak to the theme of twenty-first century capitalism? My
answer is that I shall be considering the prospects for
capitalism from what might be called a perspective of
future-related understanding. As we will see, this is very
different from the perspective of prediction. Suppose, for
example, that we looked down at the spectrum of today's
capitalisms from this new and as yet unexplained vantage
point. We would immediately see something that would
probably never enter our minds if we were interested in
forecasting which countries would be leaders and which
laggards in 2025. It is the remarkable fact that although
Japanese, Swedes, Americans, Canadians, or for that
matter, the French, the Germans, the English, and Ital-
ians, do not have the same habits or customs, do not
agree about many political means or ends, largely lack a
common sense of humor or even of civic duty, they can
nonetheless carry on an extremely important, demand-
ing, and complex common task with surprising
unanimity of understanding and purpose: they can do
business together. That is, they can transact exchanges in

the marketplace, negotiate around the bargaining table, or engage in board-room conferences as persons who see at least one aspect of life in much the same way. That aspect concerns the manner in which economic life is organized.

Looking at capitalism from this unaccustomed perspective puts into our hands a way of thinking about the future that we would not have if we approached the problem from the viewpoint of one country, even one that we know very well. The difference is that we become aware of capitalism as a system with a basic orientation discoverable in all its individual national embodiments. Only by becoming aware of this orientation can we hope to discover whether there is a logic at work behind the movement of things—a logic that enables us to think about twenty-first century capitalism in terms that will be relevant whether we are citizens of the United States, Sweden, or Japan. The predictions we all make, like the hopes and fears we all entertain, will not necessarily be any more accurate for being based on such an understanding, but they are much less likely to be wrong or misguided in the sense that they have overlooked the requirements of all capitalist systems, and therefore of any of them.

Thus, an attempt to rise above capitalism should help us think about what twenty-first century economic society might become, while still remaining capitalist; and it will help us think about where our own country might lie within even wider boundaries of historic possibility.

II

But we cannot indulge ourselves in such an exercise of imagination until we have performed a more immediate investigation. This is to make ourselves more familiar with what capitalism looks like from this distanced vantage point. I propose to do so by looking at a part of the world that is unmistakably not capitalist, and then by asking a very odd question about it. I have chosen the society of the !Kung*—the so-called Bush people of the Kalahari desert of South Central Africa, whom we visit at the moment when Gai, a Bushman hunter, has just brought down a gemsbok with a well-aimed arrow and is about to divide up the kill. The anthropologist Elizabeth Marshall Thomas describes the scene in her classic account of the !Kung people:

Gai owned two hind legs and a front leg, Tsetchwe had meat from the back, Ukwane had the other front leg, his wife had one of the feet and the stomach, the young boys had lengths of intestine. Twikwe had received the head and Dasina the udder.

It seems very unequal when you watch Bushmen divide the kill, yet it is their system, and in the end no person eats more than any other. That day Ukwane gave Gai still another piece because Gai was his relation, Gai gave meat to Dasina because she was his wife's brother. . . . No one, of course, contested Gai's large share, because he had been the hunter and by their law that much belonged to him. No one doubted that he would

---

*The exclamation mark denotes the "click" language of the people.

share his large amount with others, and they were not wrong, of course; he did.[3]

Now for the odd question I mentioned earlier: *Does one need a knowledge of economics to understand what is going on here?* Of course we need to know a great deal about the specific culture of the !Kung—their customs and beliefs, patterns of family relationship, and the like. But economics? Perhaps I can make the question less odd by turning it around. Let us suppose that a group of the !Kung somehow arranged a return journey under the guidance of an anthropologist friend who brought them to visit New York, Paris, or wherever. Would they need a knowledge of economics to understand what they saw in these strange places?

This time the question is much easier to answer. I am sure we would agree that life in a Western city would be incomprehensible without some understanding of economics—I do not mean the stuff of textbooks, or even the ability to understand the financial pages, much less the front pages of newspapers. I mean a general comprehension of what is meant by "work" and the rights it confers to remuneration, or a familiarity with the purpose of those disks and paper rectangles called "money," or some vague idea of why the numbers of disks or paper rectangles required to take possession of the very same item may change from one day to the next. All these commonplace things would be utterly mysterious to

3. Elizabeth Marshall Thomas, *The Harmless People,* New York, Vintage, 1958, pp. 49–50.

someone who came from a primitive society. There is no "work" performed among the !Kung, although of course there is a great deal of toil, because work implies complex legal and social arrangements that are completely absent in a primitive culture;[4] there are no "incomes" in our social and legal sense of the term; and of course there is no idea of money and therefore of prices. At this very basic level, then, there is as little need for a knowledge of economics to understand Kalahari life as there is an indispensable need for it in New York or Paris.

The odd question now begins to point toward our central inquiry into the nature of capitalism. Why is there no "economics" in !Kung society, whereas economics seems to pervade life in Western countries? The answer cannot be that Kalahari people do not carry on the fundamental activities of production and distribution that are universal prerequisites for survival. Primitive societies perform the tasks necessary for their maintenance and continuance exactly as do the most advanced societies—the !Kung sustain their bodies, replenish their households, repair or build their shelters, make tools and implements, embark on long and arduous journeys. If we say that there is no obvious economics in Kalahari society, we mean that there is no distinct body of knowledge required to understand their economic life. Once we know about their culture, their politics, and their technology, nothing remains to be explained with regard to their "economy."

To understand why we sometimes do, and sometimes

---

4. See "The World of Work" in my *Behind the Veil of Economics,* New York, Norton, 1988.

do not, need to know something called "economics" we must embark on one more journey of the imagination. This time we do so by turning the pages of an immense historical atlas that describes the thousands of recognizably different societies in human history, all of which, of necessity, have coped with the problems of producing and distributing the wherewithal for their continuance. In this atlas, the societies in which we will recognize the telltale characteristics of capitalism are but a tiny handful, grouped in the last pages of the book. Here, finally, economics jumps to the fore as a kind of understanding without which these societies' solution to the problem of production and distribution would be incomprehensible. Here we also glimpse the special characteristics of the "history" that conceals its lessons from us.

III

Turning the pages of this atlas is interesting for two reasons. First, we are struck by the extraordinary variety of ways in which human communities have wrestled with what we might call The Economic Problem. From one society to the next, great differences are visible in the means of selecting those who will go into the fields to hunt and gather, and those who will not—gender, family, race, punishment, ambition. Tremendous variations have marked the portions distributed to different members, and classes of members, of society, and equally great differences can be found in the explanation of these differences between the favored and the unfavored.

The second interesting aspect of the atlas of societies is the opposite of the first. It is not the variety, but the astonishing paucity of overall solutions to the problem of assuring society's material continuance. For all its variety, the atlas itself is organized into only three major sections. We have already seen an example of the first of the three divisions in the Kalahari people. How do the !Kung—and by extension, the overwhelming majority of all human societies of which we have any historical knowledge—solve the problem of producing their needed food and other requirements, and how do they distribute what they have produced in such fashion that this social effort can go on?

Direct observation quickly yields the answer. From their infancy !Kung children are taught the skills they will need and the roles they will fulfill as they accompany their elders on journeys of gathering or hunting. The essential task of training a labor force therefore takes place as part of a process of socialization, a process to which all humans must submit if they are to become acceptable members of the community. In primitive societies like the !Kung, the ruling principle of socialization is obedience to age-old ways, which is why we speak of such an organization of production and distribution as an economy under the guidance of Tradition.

From the viewpoint of our inquiry, however, there is an important point to be made with respect to this most ancient, durable, and perhaps ultimately life-preserving of all ways of overseeing the economic problem. It is that there is nothing in the socialization process that calls for the special expertise of an economist. To understand the

workings of Kalahari society we need an intimate knowledge of their culture, without which the division of Gai's
kill would be incomprehensible; we need knowledge
about how "political" decisions are made with respect to
such matters as when the community will leave one
campground for another; and we need some acquaint-
ance with their techniques of hunting and gathering if we
are to understand why the community goes about these
particular functions the way it does.

None of this, however, would ordinarily be called economic knowledge. Is there, perhaps, a deeper level of
penetration that would give us insight into an economic
motivation beneath the "surface" of society? A contemporary Western economist might suggest that such a motive can be found in a mindset that can be presupposed
behind all activities—a fundamental motivation described by economists as maximizing one's "utilities," or
satisfactions. Is this, perhaps, a key to the human nature
that we look for, out of the corner of our eye, behind
"history"? I am afraid it is a weak candidate for such a
mighty force. Perhaps a maximizing impulse drives Gai
to hunt and Dasina to gather, but to explain behavior in
this way forces us to assert that Gai's brother, who
stayed behind to laze around, was also maximizing his
utilities. An "explanation" that covers every conceivable
sort of behavior, including that which is manifestly
noneconomic, cannot tell us about behavior that is spe-
cifically "economic."

To return to my odd question, this does not mean that
there is no "economics" in the organization of primitive
social life, or that human nature is not inextricably inter-

woven into its behavioral ways. The point, rather, is that whatever motives and pressures affect production and distribution are inextricably intermixed with the cultural, political, or technological attributes of those societies. To put it differently, if we knew everything that was to be known about the social forces that shaped !Kung culture, political relationships, and technology, what would be left for an economist to find out?

In contrast to Tradition, the second great coordinative mechanism is called Command. As the name indicates, it solves the problems of production and distribution by orders from above. These may be the commands of a pharaoh or the laws of a state; on a smaller scale they may be the authority of a headman or a community council, the orders of a plantation boss or a factory manager. Command differs from Tradition in two very important ways. First, it requires an enforcement mechanism different from the internalized pressures of socialization. That mechanism is coercion—the actual or threatened use of punishment. Command backed only by the pressures of existing mores and beliefs would be no more than a form of Tradition. The orders of the Roman emperors or the Soviet commissars depended on something other than the internalized pressures of Tradition for their obedient response—indeed, they often demanded of people that they go against the routines of their past.

And what of the economics of Command? Is there such an economics, in the sense of a body of knowledge, apart from those that cover the cultures, technologies, and politics—especially politics—necessary to under-

stand the workings of ancient Egypt or the deceased Soviet Union? Taking the last case, of course we need an
understanding of the Command structure itself, in this
instance, the Soviet planning setup. In addition, we need
to be familiar with problems of running large-scale organizations, such as steel plants; and beyond that, a kind of
knowledge not previously needed—knowledge of the
problem of meshing many kinds of outputs if the blue-
print of the central planners is to be met. The collapse of
the Soviet Union has alerted us to the extraordinary difficulties of acquiring this knowledge, but the knowledge
itself is little more than the extension, on a giant scale, of
that possessed by every factory manager. This is certainly
a very important kind of knowledge, but I think we are
more likely to call it "management" than "economics."

Thus we reach the same conclusion in the case of Command societies as in those coordinated by Tradition. The
manner by which the activities of production and distribution are coordinated in both types of economic system
is so enmeshed in the culture, technology, and politics of
those kinds of societies that no special domain of knowledge remains to be filled in. Once again to make the
point, although there are assuredly economic problems
in Tradition- and Command-run societies, there is no
"economics" in either of them—no understanding that
we would lack if we fully grasped their cultures, their
technical means, and their political arrangements.

IV

And so we reach the Market. I shall leave aside for a moment the relation between the Market, as a means of organizing production and distribution, and capitalism, as the larger social order in which the Market plays a crucial role. While we are still trying to find out where economics fits into the larger picture, let us simply look at the workings of the Market through the same uncomprehending eyes as we looked at Gai distributing the parts of his gemsbok.

This time, however, let us suppose that the !Kung people, having been deeply impressed by their trip to the West, wish to create such a society for themselves. "Tell us," they ask, "is there some way we should organize ourselves to duplicate the remarkable things we have seen abroad?"

"Indeed, there is," we reply. "You must create a market economy."

"Very well," their elders agree. "What shall we instruct our people to do?"

"Aha," we answer. "The first point is that you don't tell them what to do. They do what they please. In fact, the key difference between a market economy and the economic life of a traditional community such as your own, or a command society, like that of the ancient Dahomey kingdom, is that each person in a market system will do exactly as he or she pleases."

There is considerable consternation. "You mean,"

ventures a brave elder, "that we do not tell our women to go gather fruit or our men to hunt? That we make no provision for the building and repair of our shelters? What happens then if no one goes gathering or hunting or repairs our places of rest?"

"Never fear," we reply. "All these tasks will get done. They will get done because it will be in your sisters' interests to gather, and in your brothers' interests to hunt, and in the interests of others among you to repair your shelters or to make new bows and arrows."

There are expressions of unease. "But look," says another. "Suppose we risk this astonishing change. How do we know that our gatherers will bring back the right amount of food? If it is in their interest to gather food, will they not bring back more than we need, with the result that it will spoil?"

"You don't have to worry about that," we answer. "The market system will take care of the problem. If too much food is collected, no one will want it, so its price will fall, and because it falls, it will no longer be in your sisters' interests to collect more than you need."

"Then how do we know that *enough* food will be collected?" our interrogator asks triumphantly.

"Do not fret. The market will see to that, too!"

"But what is this market that will do these wonderful things? Who runs it, for example?"

"Well, there isn't any such a *thing* as a market," we explain. "No one runs it. It's just the way people behave."

"But we thought the people behaved as they wished!"

"So they do. But you need not concern yourselves.

They will want to behave the way you want them to."

"I fear," the head person of the community says with great dignity, "that you are wasting our time. We thought you had in mind a serious proposal. What you suggest is inconceivable."[5]

V

Our depiction of what a Market society might seem like to someone who was not exactly sure what a "price" was enables us to take the last step on our roundabout journey to forming a picture of capitalism. For we now see something that is both very simple, and yet full of significance for understanding our own social order. It is that the three organizing principles of Tradition, Command, and Market impart totally different dynamics into the societies over which they hold sway.

The dynamism of the first organizing principle is very simple. It is the rule of stasis, of changelessness. This does not mean a passive surrender to fate. Many Tradition-ruled societies go on long forced marches in periods of famine and drought, and in Neolithic times we know that such communities managed the extraordinary adaptation to the demands of the Ice Age.[6] Neither does the ruling importance of Tradition impose an abject level of poverty, as we long used to believe. Anthropologist Mar-

5. Freely adapted from my *The Making of Economic Society,* 9th ed., Englewood Cliffs, N.J., Prentice-Hall, 1992, pp. 13–14.

6. See Vernon Smith, "Hunting and Gathering Societies," *The New Palgrave,* Vol. II, New York, Macmillan, 1987, pp. 695–96.

shall Sahlins has even gone so far as to call these societies "the first affluent societies," in that their established ways amply filled the expectations of their people.[7] Nonetheless, a society whose historical journey is entrusted to the guiding hand of Tradition sleepwalks through history. It may make remarkable adaptations—if it did not, human society would never have survived its danger-beset infancy—but these departures from life's well-trod course are driven by need rather than adventure or a pioneering imagination.

Things are quite different when we come to societies in which Command plays a central role in the production and allocation of their provisioning efforts. We do not know precisely when Command began to displace Tradition as a central organizing factor—the German historian Alexander Rustow has suggested that it might have begun with the neolithic descent of nomadic horsemen onto sedentary cultivators, bringing "a new breed of man, marked by a powerful superiority." Rustow believes that this formidable mounted conqueror was very likely the first ruling class; he suggests as well that it may have been the prototype of the fabled centaur.[8] These are imaginative speculations; what we know from the historical record is that in parts of the world as far separated as Egypt and Central and South America, societies appeared whose social structures resembled the phenomenal pyramids they built. Undoubtedly, such formal social hierarchies were preceded in many parts of the globe by

---

7. Marshall Sahlins, *Stone Age Economics,* New York, Aldine, 1972, Ch. 1.
8. Alexander Rustow, *Freedom and Domination,* Princeton, N. J., Princeton University Press, 1980, p. 29.

less formally stratified kinship societies.[9]

What is important for our purposes is that Command played a crucial role in the provisioning arrangements of all these societies. This is not to say that Tradition ceased to exert its steadying influence. Writing of ancient Egypt, Adam Smith notes that each person was supposed to follow the trade of his father, and would have committed some "hideous sacrilege" if he did not.[10] But the rut of Tradition could never have guided the Egyptians or the Inca or Maya in the construction of their extraordinary monuments, temples, and palaces. Neither could Tradition have provided the goods and services that sustained the armies of Alexander or Caesar, not to mention the huge military provisioning of both sides in World War II.

Command therefore interests us because it is par excellence the mode of organization required to effectuate deliberate changes in the trajectory of society. War, revolution, or any major societal undertaking—the provision of a welfare system, for instance—may utilize many of the dependable behavioral traits of Tradition and the much more flexible means of the Market, of which I shall speak next. But Command is the indispensable means of purposefully changing the ways and means of production and distribution, whether change itself originates by an imperial decree or by democratic vote.

This brings us finally to the Market—the organizing principle of capitalism. A capitalist order also depends to

---

9. See Eli Sagan, *At the Dawn of Tyranny,* New York, Knopf, 1985.
10. Adam Smith, *Wealth of Nations,* New York, Modern Library, 1937, p. 62.

no small degree on the steadying influence of Tradition—could we run a Market system without the socialized trait of honesty?—as well as on elements of Command—behind the contracts we sign are the courts that will enforce them. But it is clear that the impetus given to a Market-organized system is very different from that of Tradition or Command. If Traditional society sleepwalks through history, and Command society pursues the goals of powerful individuals or institutions, Market society is in the grip of subterranean forces that have a life of their own. Are they the forces of human nature? We will look further into that question in our next chapter.

The principle of motion imparted by these forces gives us a special kind of dynamism to which we can finally bestow the title of "economics." We are all familiar with this dynamism, whether or not we have ever read a book on the subject of economics. In its most dramatic form the dynamism has taken the form of waves of invention that have altered not only the productive capabilities of society but its social composition, even its relationship to nature itself. The first of these waves was the Industrial Revolution of the late eighteenth and early nineteenth centuries that brought the cotton mill and the steam engine, along with the mill town and mass child labor; a second revolution gave us the railroad, the steamship, and the mass production of steel, and along with them a new form of economic instability—business cycles; a third revolution introduced the electrification of life and the beginnings of a society of mass semi-luxury consumption; a fourth rode in on the automobile that changed everything from sex habits to the locations of centers of population; a fifth electronified life in our own time. This is, of course, an arbitrary listing. What was arresting about the dynamism was that change itself became the norm of daily life. Over the entire previous history of humanity, children had lived material lives that were essentially the same as those of their parents, accidents of war or natural disaster always excepted. From the mid-nineteenth century on, that sense of continuity was ever more noticeably displaced by a sense of immanent change.

The continuous remaking of the social environment is assuredly the most noticeable aspect of the Market's impact on social provisioning, but it is not the most significant. The deeper aspect of this kaleidoscopic changefulness is that it conceals a kind of orderliness. This is because the forces it unleashes work blindly but not haphazardly. Quite to the contrary, there are control mechanisms, feedbacks, and self-generated limitations built into the torrent of Market-driven change, so that as we look back on the historic trends and patterns of production and distribution, we can see that the working of a capitalist economy gives evidences of systemic patterns, of a kind of grand historic trajectory, a certain orderliness. This is, of course, a first view of the process we call progress.

What are these patterns, this orderliness, this trajectory? What are the sources of the energy, the relentless, ubiquitous pressure for change that has been capitalism's contribution to history, for worse as well as better? These are matters for our coming chapters. I must end this one on the theme with which it began—the predictability of our futures. As I said earlier, the future of any particular capitalism is marked by a very high degree of indeterminacy. But we have now seen that capitalism as a whole is unique in generating persistent and powerful tendencies to change. Paradoxically, it is this very immanent changefulness that enables us to speak about its future with a degree of analytical penetration that we cannot apply to any previous social order.

This capability derives from the behavioral patterns that a Market system imposes on its members, an aspect of capitalism that we shall repeatedly encounter in chapters to come. Suffice it to say that these patterns form the basis of the extraordinary scenarios by which the great economists have described its historical trajectory. From Adam Smith through Marx to Keynes, powerful expositions have indicated the general direction of capitalist development, anchoring their analyses in the activities to which the participants in a market system find themselves driven by their own self-interest. In no case were the scenarios capable of foreseeing the capitalist trajectory very far into the future. Nonetheless, in all cases they gave to the present a sense of being part of a process whose roots lay deep in the past—perhaps even in human nature itself—and whose unfolding lead to prospects big with significance for our progeny. Capitalism thus carries us all along into futures that are full of unpredictability, and yet formed and shaped in ways that are far from being utterly unforeseeable. Need I add that this characteristic is intimately entwined with the belief in progress that is today under such uneasy reapparaisal?

3

The Drive
for Capital

I

CAPITALISM, I HOPE we now see, is a more remarkable social order than it appears to us,
who live inside it as fish live in water. The preceding
chapter was primarily devoted to making us sense its profound differences compared with other societies dominated by Tradition and Command. Now it is time to turn
our attention exclusively to the question of what capitalism is, rather than what it isn't; and, by extension, to the
ways in which it embodies history and its lessons.

We have already noted that capitalism's most striking
historical characteristic is its extraordinary propensity
for self-generated change. If capitalism is anything, it is a
social order in constant change—and beyond that,
change that seems to have a direction, an underlying
principle of motion, a logic. Tracing the differences between the Western world of the 1700s, 1800s, 1900s, and
today we all feel a kind of developmental thrust at work
that enables us to talk about its history in different terms

than those we might use in speaking of the history of the great Asian kingdoms or the Roman Empire. In a word, the thrust of capitalist history conveys a notion of immanent change—a past leading ineluctably upward into the present, and a present promising further movement upward into the future. It is this strong feeling of self-propulsion along a rising gradient that constitutes the core of the idea of progress.

This brings us to a theme already sounded in the Introduction, where the idea of progress appears called into question by the threats and disappointments of our time. This is not yet the time to go more deeply into that possibility, but it seems very much the time to look closely into the energy that capitalism generates like a battery generates electricity. Everyone knows the source of this unique social voltage. It is the activity that lies at the heart of the order—the drive to get ahead, to make money, to accumulate capital. We will use the last phrase because, as we will see, there is an integral connection between "capital" and the system that is built on its name—a connection that is veiled, or even concealed, in the everyday terms of "getting ahead" or "making money." Our first order of business is accordingly very clear. It is to look into what we mean by the word that has become not just the name but the identifying badge of the social order in which we live.

Surprisingly, capital is not the same thing as wealth. Wealth is a very ancient aspect of human civilization, but the drive to amass it, which we can trace back to the Egyptian pharaohs, has never become a force for continuous and deep change. Egypt was much the same when

Napoleon conquered it in the early nineteenth century as it had been three thousand years earlier. In similar fashion, the Inca and Maya, or the rulers of India or China, accumulated vast treasuries of gold and built magnificent palaces and temples, but there was never anything in their long histories that even vaguely resembled the developmental logic we see in the last three hundred years of Western history. I have already said the reason: wealth is not capital.

What is wealth? We can approach the question by looking at something even older than gold hoards and majestic buildings. I have mentioned that primitive societies may have enjoyed the affluence of contentment, save when nature went against them. Let me now add that many such societies also created monuments that required lengthy and arduous labors—Stonehenge or the famous carved heads of the Easter Island, the Lascaux cave paintings or the great totem poles of the northwest coast of North America. Was this wealth? I think not. I would call such creations objects of virtue. As such, they were embodiments of the community's spiritual life—testimonies to its observance of time-honored ways, placatory offerings to an animate Nature.

Wealth is not an object of virtue. It is a symbol of power and prestige, usually accruing to the personage to whom it belongs, and to a lesser extent to the society in which it is found. The very word "belongs" tells us something about wealth that differentiates it from objects of virtue. It is that wealth is inextricably associated with inequality. This is an insight that we get from a most unlikely source, the first of the great philosophers of capitalism, who wrote that "wherever there is great property, there is great inequality. . . . The affluence of the rich supposes the indigence of the many." It is Adam Smith speaking, not Karl Marx.[11]

The matter of inequality deserves some attention. Smith was aware that the desire for riches needed explanation, and he found it in two benefits that wealth bestowed. The first was esteem, which is based on unequal status. "The rich man glories in his riches," Smith wrote, "because he feels they naturally draw upon him the attention of the world. At the thought of this, his heart seems to swell and dilate itself within him, and he is fonder of his wealth on this account, than for all the other advantages it procures him."[12] The second reason was rooted in another source of the difference that wealth introduced. "Wealth," wrote Smith, quoting Hobbes, "is power." Smith quickly goes on to say that the power conferred by wealth is not political or military, although it may be a stepping-stone to the latter. It is "the power of purchasing; a certain command over all the labour, or over all the produce of labour which is then in the market."[13]

The element of inequality here is revealed in the term "command." Smith does not mean that wealth simply allows two equally circumstanced individuals to exchange their services on a mutually satisfying basis, using money as a convenient way of simplifying the transac-

11. Smith, *Wealth,* op. cit., pp. 709–10.
12. Adam Smith, *The Theory of Moral Sentiments,* Oxford, Clarendon Press, 1976, pp. 50–51.
13. Smith, *The Wealth,* op. cit., p. 31.

tion. He means that a lack of wealth may force a less favorably circumstanced individual to enter into a disadvantageous market relation with a more favorably situated one purely because of the difference in their situations. It hardly comes as a surprise that the rich are in a position to enjoy a disproportionately large share of society's goods and services. What may come as an unaccustomed thought is that the very concept of wealth implies such an inequality, and that a society of equals-in-wealth, even though it enjoyed the pleasures of the Arabian Nights, would of necessity be a society in which there was no economic power.

This brings us to an aspect of ownership that has special importance for capitalism. It is the inequality between the owners of the means of production and those who work with those means—that is, between capitalists and "their" workers. Looking back for a moment at Kalahari society, we can doubtless find a degree of inequality among the personal effects or weapons owned by various members of the community. But the idea that a rich Bushman might own all the tribe's weapons, so that Gai would have to rent his bow and arrow to feed his family, or that he might even have to become an "employee" of the rich Bushman in order to feed himself would be as unthinkable to the Kalahari as it would be to us if anyone in our society could walk into a factory and make free use of the equipment that was there. It is the right to deny access to the means of production that is the central advantage conferred by wealth in capitalism. An individual who owns no capital is perfectly free to labor as he or she wishes, and may in fact, became very successful using only the property of his or her body—actors or singers, as instances in point. But anyone who has no such personal talent must pay for the privilege of making use of wealth that belongs to another. This puts into an unaccustomed light the institution of "wage labor," which is the manner in which the labor of individuals is marshalled and remunerated under capitalism.

II

Is capital wealth? Yes and no. Capital is certainly wealth, insofar as one who possesses capital is usually a person who enjoys esteem and who wields power in the marketplace. The question, then, is whether wealth is capital. The disconcerting answer is that sometimes it is and sometimes it is not.

The difference lies in the peculiar nature of capital. Capital is wealth whose value does not inhere in its physical characteristics but in its use to create a larger amount of capital. Typically, this use takes place as money is converted into commodities such as raw materials, the raw materials converted into finished goods and services, and the finished goods sold on the market—not to make a profit and retire to a life of ease, but to buy more raw materials to start the process over again. As a consequence of this endless turnover, the physical characteristics of commodities have nothing to do with their function as a means to wealth: a capitalist can get rich on coal or scrap metal, which no one could imagine as wealth. By the same token, a Rembrandt painting, which is certainly an embodiment of wealth, does not become capital unless it is no longer wanted for itself, but is used as a stepping-stone for amassing still more capital. Then the possessor of the Rembrandt becomes an art dealer. Capital thus differs from wealth in its intrinsically dynamic character, continually changing its form from commodity into money and then back again, in an endless metamorphosis that already makes clear its integral connection with the changeful nature of capitalism itself.

What drives this process that Marx called the self-expansion of capital? At this focal point of our analysis, understanding becomes uncertain. Economists speak of the never-ending expansion process as reflecting the drive to "maximize utilities," a view of which I spoke skeptically in the previous chapter. The vague motive of "maximizing" our satisfactions seems inadequate to account for the insatiability of the drive that Marx described as "Accumulate! Accumulate! That is Moses and the prophets."[14] Somewhere between the two is Adam Smith's assertion that we are the creatures of a "desire of bettering our condition"—a desire that he said "comes with us from the womb, and never leaves us till we go into the grave"—and his further description of the most common object of this desire as an "augmentation of fortune," which is to say, making money.[15]

I think myself that the unappeasable appetite for expanding capital is better understood as a manifestation of those drives that in earlier societies took the form of illimitable expansions of empire or a godlike glorification

---

14. Karl Marx, *Capital,* New York, International Publishers, 1967, p. 595.
15. Smith, *Wealth,* op. cit., p. 324.

of kings. The empty maximizing of utilities and the rather mild "bettering our condition" by making money then take on their necessary urgency by linking the drive to amass wealth with unconscious motives, probably derived from infantile fantasies of omnipotence. We will see in a moment why, in our society, these fantasies take the form of an expansion of capital.

But there is a second motive that supplements and perhaps exacerbates the first. It is that the consequence of each capitalist seeking to expand his scope of operations soon leads to the collision of capitalist against capitalist that we call competition. "One capitalist always kills many," said Marx.[16] Thus there is an element of the spirit of war—partly aggressive, partly defensive—added to that of sheer aggrandizement. From this viewpoint, capitalism appears not merely as a social order characterized by constant change, but as one in which the pursuit of wealth fulfills some of the same unconscious purposes as did military glory and personal majesty in an earlier time.

III

These reflections again connect the study of capitalism with the insistent and disturbing questions raised by our current historical situation. One of these questions, as we have already mentioned, is the role of human nature as the moving force behind events. Insofar as we often hear that the profit motive is an expression of human nature,

---

16. Marx, *Capital,* op. cit., Vol. I, p. 763.

one would think that we could find the accumulation of capital in all societies, including those organized under the aegis of Tradition and Command. Yet we hear little about it before capitalism appears on the scene in the eighteenth century.

We have already seen the reason. Wealth is not the same thing as capital. Julius Caesar was given the governorship of Spain with its great mines, from which he returned in a few years a wealthy man but not a capitalist. The appearance of capital as a driving, transforming social process required more than the enrichment of successful generals. For one thing, economic life had to be raised from the low regard in which it was held—"devoid of nobility, and hostile to perfection of character," in the words of Aristotle—to something approaching respectability. As part of this process, a semi-independent "economy" had to be wrenched free of the enveloping state. And underlying the whole, a web of transactions had to be enlarged until it reached into the very life processes of society itself. Until the most fundamental activities of production were brought within the circuit of transforming money into commodities and commodities back into more money, a capitalist social order could not take root. Only then could the accumulation of capital inherit the fantasies of power that earlier fastened on exploits of glory and adventure. Thus, however much "maximizing" or "bettering our condition" or sheer aggressiveness or acquisitiveness reflect attributes of human nature, they seem to have played passive rather an active roles in the ascension of capitalism. No doubt the drive for accumulation could not have insinuated itself so deeply and widely into behavior had it not lent itself easily to the primal needs and appetites of the human personality, but there is also no doubt that those needs and appetites, in themselves, have been insufficient to produce a capitalist order in the absence of immense impersonal happenings.

That immense impersonal happening, in the case of capitalism, was the fall of the Roman Empire, a catastrophic "event" that stretched out over some four hundred years. The fall of Rome was crucial not only because the social hierarchy of the empire was at every level incompatible with a capitalist order, but because its shattered ruins provided an extraordinary setting in which such an order would emerge—slowly, painfully, and without any sense of fulfilling a historic mission—during the thousand-year period we call feudalism. The often-noted failure of capitalism to appear spontaneously more than once in world history is likely due to the fact that this social setting has never appeared elsewhere.

We can only trace the barest narrative of that thousand-year birthing process. The disappearance of the empire left Europe without unifying law, currency, and government, broken into a crazy quilt of isolated and self-dependent towns, manorial estates, and petty fiefdoms—a catastrophe like that of the collapse of the Soviet Union, magnified a hundredfold. It was, however, the very fragmentation of feudal life that paved the way for the transformation that followed. By the ninth century—four hundred years after the "fall" began—a few pack trains of merchants from what was left of the old Roman workshops were beating their way from one manor to the next, accompanied by armed retinues to fend off attacks by robber barons. Gradually these merchant adventurers insinuated themselves into the affairs of the manor and especially the town, so that by the fourteenth century—we are now almost a thousand years into medieval history—their descendants had become the political authorities of expanding "burgh" or urban life. Here they played a role that was both indispensable for the evolving feudal order and ultimately subversive of it: essential because the feudal rulers were continually forced to turn for loans to their resident burghers, some of whom were by now very rich; subversive because the commercial way of life for which the lenders stood was ultimately incompatible with feudal dominance. By the end of the seventeenth century a bourgeois (burgher) class was already a political power in England, by the end of the eighteenth century it was the real master of France, by the end of the nineteenth century, the dominant political force in the world.

With the coming to power of the bourgeoisie, there arose as well the lineaments of a new social order in which new money-minded values were perhaps the most noticeable aspect, but the spread of a new form of economic life was by far the most important. In the country, the institution of serfdom, in which the serf paid a portion of his crop to his lord and kept the rest for himself, gave way to a quite different institution in which a capitalist farmer paid his hands a wage, but owned the whole of the product they brought forth. In the town, the relationship of master and apprentice, under the strict supervision of guild rules, became that of employer and worker, under no regulation save the marketplace for labor. In the big cities, money-making moved from the suspect periphery of life to its esteemed center.

Thus the institutions of feudalism disappeared, not without bloodshed, and in their place appeared those of an order that Adam Smith called the "Society of Perfect Liberty." The name referred to economic, not political, freedom, and by our standards the degree of freedom was very far from perfect. Nonetheless, in a Society of Perfect Liberty workers could move freely from one location or occupation to another, which as serfs and apprentices they could not; and capitalists could raise or lower their prices as they saw fit, which as guild members they could not. Thus the institutions, if not yet the name of capitalism, took shape. As the term denoting the water in which we swim, "capitalism" entered the English language sometime in the middle of the nineteenth century, perhaps in Thackeray's work, of all places! It has been with us ever since, although its checkered past and problematic future incline some to prefer "free private enterprise system" with its more upbeat connotation.

IV

The emplacement of capital accumulation as the moving force of the new social order makes clear why capitalism revolutionizes material and social life in a manner that imperial kingdoms, for all their pyramids, hoards of gold, or fantastic palaces, did not. The reason is that the drive for capital is directed at the foundation of society, not at its apex. The continuous conversion of commodities into money is most readily achieved across the broad spectrum of production, where it acts as a powerful force to augment the quantity and change the quality of output. The amassing of wealth in the form of monuments and treasuries has no such effect.

Adam Smith made this expansion of production a central feature of a Society of Perfect Liberty. Expansion begins, as Smith explains, because the most readily available means for a capitalist to better his condition is to save a portion of his profits and invest it in additional equipment, thereby adding to the potential output of his enterprise, and thus to his future income. In the famous opening pages of *Wealth,* Smith describes how the process works in a small pin "manufactory" employing only ten men. By dividing the manufacturing process into separate steps, each performed by a separate person, often aided by machinery, the ten workers were able to make more than forty-eight thousand pins in a day: "if they had all wrought separately and independently," observes Smith, ". . . they certainly could not each of them have made twenty, perhaps not one pin in a day."[17]

The accumulation process thus exerts its immediate impact on the social environment by multiplying the productivity of labor. Smith explains the increase by the encouragement of the workman's "dexterity," the saving of time previously lost in "sauntering" from one task to another, and the more ready mechanization of "divided" labor. All this leads to the enlargement of output that is a

---

17. Smith, *Wealth,* op. cit., pp. 4–5.

central achievement of Smith's society. Less well known is that Smith expected that process of growth to come to a halt as soon as society had built all the capital it needed. Behind this vision of salvation is the presumption that output increases, but the product remains the same. It is characteristic of Smith's lack of interest in technological or organizational change that he expressed little confidence in the managerial capabilities of the "joint-stock" enterprises that were beginning to appear.[18]

In the vision that has largely displaced it—one associated with the work of Joseph Schumpeter in the 1930s—the descendant of Smith's manufacturer soon finds the market for pins glutted, but discovers another means of expanding his capital by varying his product, perhaps producing pins with colored heads. Thereafter, his son takes a chance on a new invention called "safety" pins; his grandson moves into paper clips; their descendants take the leap into zippers and Velcro. My illustration draws on the Victorian image of family capitalism, but Schumpeter's insight was that the most formidable means of capital accumulation was the displacement of one process or product by another at the hands of giant enterprise. He called the process "creative destruction," and it remains the central agency of change in all advanced capitalist economies.

Whether carried out by Smith's pin factory or Schumpeter's innovating corporation, accumulation changes the larger society in two ways. There is no mistaking the

---

18. Smith, *Wealth,* op. cit., pp. 94–95, 700. See also my "Paradox of Progress: Decline and Decay" in *Essays on Adam Smith,* ed., A.S. Skinner and T. Wilson, Oxford, Clarendon Press, 1975.

single most important. It is the elevation of living standards in those countries in which capitalism's complex structure successfully takes root. A calculation by the demographer Paul Bairoch makes the point vividly. He compares the changes in per capita GNP, in constant dollars, between the "presently developed" and the "presently less developed" countries—that is, between the capitalist and noncapitalist worlds—for the 1750s and the 1980s.[19] Looking at the comparative performance of the two sets of countries we see that whereas their average living standards were much the same in the 1750s—in itself an astonishing fact—over the next 230 years the average person in the capitalist world became eight times richer than one in the noncapitalist world.

One should, of course, regard these figures with some caution. One reason for the extraordinary difference in performance is the rapid movement toward population stabilization in the advanced countries, compared with its runaway growth in the underdeveloped world. Both the stabilization and the explosion of population may be indirect effects of capitalism—the first reflecting its spreading middle-class culture, the latter testifying to the powerful efficacy of its advances in public health, introduced into nations without birth control. Some portion of the divergence in income, in other words, is undoubtedly the result of side effects of capitalism rather than its superior productive performance alone. A more important reason was the drainage of wealth from the underdeveloped Periphery to the developed Center—a capital-

---

19. Paul Bairoch in Just Faaland, *Population and the World Economy in the 21st Century,* Oxford, Basil Blackwell, 1982, p. 192.

ist version of a much older imperialist exploitation of the weak by the strong. The widening gulf between rich and poor nations is undoubtedly not just a measure of the superior performance of the capitalist world but also an indication of its exploitative powers.

Thus one must undoubtedly qualify the message that Bairoch's figures convey. That is not, however, to deny their striking conclusion. Capitalism has altered the course of history first and foremost by creating an entirely new socioeconomic environment in which, for the first time, material conditions have improved steadily and markedly in those areas where the system flourished. I make the point once more for emphasis. Looking back over 150 years of growth in the United States we find that real per capita income up to the mid 1980s grew at an average rate of 1.5 percent a year—perhaps not very impressive-sounding, until we realize that this was enough to double real living standards every forty-seven years. Moreover, with the exception of the bottom years of the depression of 1869 and the terrible early 1930s, economic activity in every year has been within ten percent of a straight line linking 1839 and 1985.[20] More recently, we have seen this same transformative process take root in Europe and, more recently yet, in Japan and along the Pacific Rim in Taiwan, Korea, Hong Kong, perhaps Singapore and Malaysia.

---

20. *Economic Report of the President,* Washington, D.C., 1986.

V

Writing in the midst of a serious economic deterioration whose onset can already be discerned within the final years of the long trajectory of growth, it is difficult to think of capitalism as a social order whose principal achievement has been the improvement of material life. But it is this very slowdown that brings home the importance of the secular expansion of the past, not alone as a base from which to appraise capitalist prospects for the future, but as the source of an idea whose importance is all the more strongly felt as its presence seems to wane. This is again the idea of progress—an idea absent from any social order preceding capitalism, and one that would assuredly be jeopardized by any lasting doubts concerning the ability to accumulate capital.

The link between accumulation and material progress is not, however, a simple one. The reader of the *Communist Manifesto* is always surprised to discover that it contains a veritable paean to the powers of the accumulation process. The reader also discovers that the process, like everything in Marx, is dialectical, two-sided, contradictory. From the beginning, the elevation of material well-being brought about by the successful development of capitalism has been accompanied by a new form of social misery—not the ancient scourges of bad crops, invasion by marauders, or simple injustice, but an "economic" side effect that had no precursors in earlier societies. This was the tendency of the growth process to generate both wealth and misery simultaneously, as part of the workings of the accumulation process itself.

The new form of misery made its initial appearance in Elizabethan England as the "enclosures" of land. Enclosures meant that land traditionally available as a "commons," where poor peasants could build their huts, graze their beasts, and grow a few vegetables, was now taken over by its legal owners, mainly landed gentry, for the exclusive use of sheep grazing. The enclosures themselves were approved by Parliament and were accompanied by small payments to the peasants who were dispossessed. But they exacted a hideous price. Returning from a tour of her realm, Queen Elizabeth exclaimed that "paupers were everywhere"; a hundred and fifty years years later, the "wandering poor," as the uprooted peasants were then being called, were still the scandal of the nation. The cause of this massive and long-lasting misery lay squarely in the introduction of capitalist processes into a still largely feudal society. Enclosures were undertaken because the sale of wool had become a profitable activity. The wool trade was without question one of the growth centers of late seventeenth-century England—it is not for nothing that the Lord Chancellor of the House of Commons today sits on a woolsack. Thus, considerations of "economics" both quickened the pulse of production and became a cause for disruption and impoverishment.

The two-edged process took a different guise a century later. By that time, the active centers of accumulation had moved to the manufactories about which Smith wrote. The outputs of these burgeoning industries undoubtedly benefitted the middle-class consumers who

bought them, and the profits they earned certainly benefitted their owners. What is not so certain is whether benefits also accrued to the workmen. Their wages were low,
but that was the case everywhere, so that was not the
specific ill introduced by capitalism. Smith himself identified the ill as the effects of the repetitious, mindless tasks
to which the division of labor led. "[T]he man whose
whole life is spent in performing a few operations,"
Smith complained, ". . . has no occasion to exercise his
understanding . . . and generally becomes as stupid and
ignorant as it is possible for a human creature to
become."[21]

By the early nineteenth century the still small-scale
manufactories were eclipsed by the "dark Satanic mills"
where women and children labored under brutal conditions for less than subsistence pay. This underside of
Dickensian England is well known, although it is not so
often remarked that the same mills that appalled the
more sensitive observers of the day were also centers of
accumulation on a major scale, as well as one of the first
sources of its overseas reach. Frederick Engels remarked
to someone that he had never seen so ill-built a city as
Manchester, with its hideous slums. His companion lis-
tened quietly, and then said, "And yet there is a great
deal of money made here; good day, sir."[22]

We will return later to the question of the side effects of
accumulation: it is enough to mention the problem of
ecological damage caused by industrial processes to

21. Smith, *Wealth,* op. cit., p. 734.
22. From Edmund Wilson, *To The Finland Station,* New York, Farrar,
Straus, & Giroux, 1972, p. 142.

make clear that the negative aspect of the accumulation of capital is by no means a matter of past history. But in this initial consideration of the drive for capital, I want to introduce a second manner in which accumulation reveals its power to cut two ways. This is to link the drive for capital with the recurrent tendency of the economy to lose its forward momentum, even to go into reverse.

We have already noted that Smith rather naively expected a Society of Perfect Liberty to go into decline once it had built all the manufactories for which there would be a need. After Smith's time, interest focused less on this grand vision of rise and fall and turned to the question of whether a commercial society had a tendency, from time to time, to develop "general gluts." This then evolved into the concept of business "cycles"—self-generated tendencies to swing between periods of expansion and contraction, for which many underlying causes were suggested—recurrent credit shortages, overshoots and mismatches of supply and demand, swings of optimism and pessimism. For a while, during the 1920s and 1930s, there was a flurry of interest, perhaps sparked by the advent of the inexplicable Great Depression, in the possibility of "long waves" that imposed a majestic fifty-year rhythm of expansion followed by exhaustion, but no wholly satisfactory explanation was ever offered for the existence of the waves in the first place.

In our own time, attention has mainly been directed toward explaining the process of growth itself. I recall a class from my college days in the 1930s when Alvin Hansen, John Maynard Keynes's first apostle in the United States, looked with interest at an upward-sloping wavy line on the blackboard depicting the succession of business cycles over time, and remarked that the bottom of one depression was often higher than the top of a boom two or three cycles back. Hansen was stumbling onto the idea of changes in the rate of growth, not in their cyclical pattern, as the fundamental problem in the instability of the system.

Two interesting hypotheses have been put forward in recent years to account for the irregularity of this long-term trajectory. The first explains it in terms of generational shifts in the "social structure of accumulation" that determines the relative strengths of labor and capital. This social structure begins with the state of union-management relationships, extends into the interaction of business and government, and thence into the general realm of public opinion—all elements that enter into the balance of power between labor and capital, and thereby affect the wage rate, a key variable in determining the rate of investment.[23] The second hypothesis emphasizes the irregular appearance of "transformational" technological or institutional breakthroughs that open up vast investment frontiers, such as the periods of railroadization or automobilization mentioned in our previous chapter.[24] In turn, both these explanations of changes in the rate of economic growth can be loosely tied to changing configurations in the overall form of capitalism from a mercantile to an industrial system, and now to a post-

---

23. See David Gordon, Richard Edwards, and Michael Reich, *Segmented Work, Divided Workers,* New York, Cambridge University Press, 1982.
24. Edward J. Nell, *Transformational Growth and Effective Demand,* New York, Macmillan, 1992.

industrial and multinational structural basis.

Do these hypotheses cast light on the prospects for accumulation in the future? Of course, they alert us to the political balance of power and the transformational effects of technology as key elements in determining the rate of economic growth. Unfortunately, that awareness does not add much to our capacity to anticipate the future with any degree of assurance. It is possible—or better, perhaps, it is not impossible—that the coming decades will witness a series of massive technological stimuli of the kind that have propelled us forward with irregular regularity over the last two centuries, most recently in the twenty-five-year postwar boom in which tourism became the largest single industry in the world, and computerization changed the organization of every business from the dry cleaner to the megacorporation. Alas, the same can be said for a drearier possibility, namely that the future will be dominated by periods of stagnation and decline, most recently manifested in the decade-long stagnation in growth, decline in productivity, and rise in unemployment in virtually all capitalist nations. The same indeterminate prospect faces us with respect to the social structure within which capitalist accumulation takes place. The decades ahead may see a new political "entente" such as that of the 1950s, which put into place the hugely stimulative institutions of the welfare state; or it may witness the serious erosion of the belief in, and efficacy of, that social structure, similar to that of the 1980s.

Thus the long-term prospects for growth remain opaque, as they always have been. Whether there may yet

be possibilities for attaining transformational momentum, even if the spontaneous processes are laggard, is a
matter we will come to in due course. But I cannot end
this chapter as I would dearly like, with a plausible fore-
cast, optimistic or otherwise, of the prospects for continued capitalist expansion. Instead, I must remind my
readers of the much more modest ambition that moti-
vates this book. It is to understand better the nature of
the system in which we live, and thereby the boundaries
within which any feasible prospect for capitalism will
have to lie. To have grasped the power, the necessity, and
the vulnerability of the drive to accumulate capital is already to have learned something about the futures we
can imagine for the twenty-first century; and as a consequence, to have prepared ourselves, in some measure, for
history's visitations.

4

The Politics
of Capitalism

I

THE PREVIOUS CHAPTER was about capitalism as an economic system; this one will be about capitalism as a political order. The difference between the two is not as great as we might think—we have already seen that the life process of capital expansion has political as well as economic consequences, generating social ills alongside material well-being. Marx, who was surely a searching diagnostician of its political as well as economic system, thought that the economics of capitalism was dominated by the "contradictions" generated by its drive for production, and its politics by the "class struggles" stemming from its mode of distribution.

The idea of class struggle sounds stilted today, the vocabulary of another era. But Marx's perception should not be written off too quickly. Although it may lie in the background, out of sight, a tension between those who occupy the favored positions and those who do not informs the politics of all stratified social orders. That is

67

only to say that the fundamental political issue of capitalism, as of every stratified society, concerns its class relations.

We will return to this issue toward the end of this inquiry. But meanwhile, if we ask what is the immediate central political issue in capitalism—the issue that takes on an often obsessive prominence in every capitalist nation—there is no question where to look. It is the relationship between business and government, or from our more distant perspective, between the economy and the state.

We often fail to realize how remarkable is this aspect of capitalist political life. This is because we are not generally aware how unique is the separation of overall governance in any social order into two independent and legally divorced realms that are at the same time mutually dependent and married for life. The closest analog to this cleaving of the capitalist order is the division in feudalism between the authority of the Church and the State, but the frictions of that relationship are dwarfed beside those of the divided secular authority within a capitalist society.

Let me start, then, by saying a word about each side of this divide. We are all aware of the difference between "the state," with its institutions of law and order, its apparatus of force, and its ceremonial functions, and "the economy," with its factories and stores, banks and markets, want ads and unemployment offices. It is the business of the state to govern and that of the economy to produce and distribute. We recognize that to some extent governing requires that the state lay down rules and regu-

lations for the economy, and that the state must intervene into economic affairs on occasion; and we know as
well that economic affairs inescapably intrude on the
governing function, sometimes in ways that are antitheti-
cal to the public interest—foreign policy as an instance in
point—and sometimes in ways that are inseparable from
it—the formulation of economic policy as the central
case.

What we do not ordinarily bear in mind is that this
duality of realms, with its somewhat smudgy boundaries,
has no counterpart in noncapitalist societies. In the centrally planned socialisms, for instance, there was, of
course, only one realm, save for peasants' plots and a tiny
"sector" of street trade. More important, there was only
one realm even in such seemingly capitalist-like societies
as ancient Greece, with its flourishing international
trade, or Rome, which sported a kind of stock market in
the forum, or sixteenth-century Florence with its monied
life. The reason was that the governing authority of the
state was legally unbounded. The idea that the material
provisioning of society, gladly left to the self-motivated
activities of farmers, artisans, and merchants, was not in
some ultimate sense under the authority of the state
would never have occurred to Aristotle or Cicero or Ma-
chiavelli. If the state did not much meddle in these activities it was because it had more important things to do,
such as the conduct of war and the celebration of its own
majesty, and because these "economic" tasks were sufficiently routinized, or marginal, to be left to themselves.
Thus, to sound again a theme that runs through all these
pages, there was no economy in precapitalist societies for

the same reasons that there was no economics. To be sure, all the necessary activities of production and distribution were in evidence, but they were in no way subject to a different social discipline from their larger social and political functions.

The separation begins, as we have already seen, in the political rubble of the collapsed Roman Empire, where we glanced at the rise of the merchant class from a useful but incongruous presence in the medieval landscape to a social "estate" capable of challenging, and in the end taking precedence over, the aristocratic world around it. This time, however, I want to stress another aspect of that epoch-marking change. It is to call to our attention the two-sided political outcome of the economic birthing process. On the one hand, a true realm of power and authority came into existence in a network of farms, household industries, and trading links that for the first time considered itself out from under the thumb of the state and capable of managing its own affairs with a minimum of political guidance or restraint—a kind of state within a state. On the other hand, the newly constituted economic realm was by no means ready to abandon its close relationships with—even its dependency on—the older political realm.

What we have, then, is the emergence of a social order at once divided and united. The obvious problem posed by such a division of authority was what should be the duties of each realm, and as usual, Adam Smith caught the issue precisely in his celebration of a Society of Perfect Liberty. He begins by emphasizing the newly won independence of its economic "half":

Every man, as long as he does not violate the laws of justice, is left perfectly free to pursue his own interest his own way, and to bring both his industry and his capital into competition with those of any other man, or order of men. The sovereign [we can read "the state"] is completely discharged from a duty, in the attempting to perform which he must always be exposed to innumerable delusions, and for the proper performance of which no human wisdom or knowledge could ever be sufficient—the duty of superintending the industry of private people and of directing it toward the employments most suitable to the interest of society.

In the very next sentence, however, Smith goes on to describe three duties "of great importance" that the state must still perform. They are, first, "the duty of protecting the society from violence and invasion"; second, "the duty of protecting, as far as possible, every member of the society from the injustice or oppression of every other member of it"; and third, "the duty of erecting and maintaining certain public works and certain public institutions, which it can never be to the interest of any individual, or group of individuals, to erect and maintain because the profit would never repay the expence . . . though it may frequently do much more than repay it to a great society."[25]

As usual, Smith is impressive because he is so even-handed. He rails against the "impertinences" of meddlesome officials who seek to substitute their own wishes for those of the market. Yet his powerful desire to give private industry its head does not prevent him from recognizing that government has an indispensable role to play.

---

25. Smith, *Wealth*, op. cit., p. 651. I have slightly altered punctuation for ease of reading.

Moreover, by describing its duties in broad functional terms, Smith by no means prescribes narrow limits on its role. Putting flesh and blood on the three public duties described above gives us the defense departments and ministries of capitalism, with their multifarious economic and political webs of influence; the national systems of law and order, with their courts, police forces, and jails; and the necessity to "erect and maintain" what we would call the national infrastructure, explicitly including education, which Smith esteemed highly. This is certainly not a welfare state, of which we shall hear more shortly, but neither is it, by any stretch of the imagination, a kind of capitalist anarchy.

II

The two realms of capitalism establish the framework for its political life. They also establish the framework for an aspect of capitalism that is much celebrated, but rarely connected with this bifurcated structure. This is the political freedom that already distinguished capitalist society from the imperial kingdoms that were its initial rivals, and that separated it even more decisively from the centralized socialism that was until recently its arch competitor. Our next task, accordingly, is to inquire into the ways in which the division of power between two realms connects with the idea of freedom. This will lead us once again to consider the drive for capital that energizes the system, but from a quite different vantage point.

Is there a linkage between this drive and the enjoyment

of freedom? One famous argument is that the very pursuit of wealth is, in itself, an expression of an absolutely basic freedom on which all kinds of liberty are founded. That basic freedom was first described by John Locke in his famous *Second Treatise on Government,* published in 1690, as the right of individuals to own their own bodies and, by a small extension, the labor of their bodies. Adam Smith, following Locke, called this "the most sacred and inviolable" of all forms of property.[26] From this initial assertion of the right of individuals to command their own labor, Locke moved to the justification of the private ownership of those things that individuals appropriated from nature by that labor; and by a seeming small, but actually very great extension, he further justified their ownership of the things that their "servants" appropriated for them. The right to command one's labor thus established for Locke the essential area of freedom that guards the individual against the arbitrary incursion of society. As C.B. Macpherson has shown, Locke's argument also extends that conception of freedom to cover the "possessive individualism" that becomes the linchpin of an acquisitive society.[27] Capitalism itself thus appears to be a social order that is both the embodiment and the expression of freedom.

It is easy to dismiss this linkage of liberty to the right to acquire wealth as mere privilege parading as morality, and it is no great feat to uncover the oppressions and unfreedoms that have been imposed in the name of the

---

26. Smith, *Wealth,* op. cit., pp. 121–22.
27. C.B. Macpherson, *The Theory of Possessive Individualism,* New York, Oxford University Press, 1962.

property "rights" that follow from this view of freedom. I would nonetheless propose that we consider sympathetically the idea that there is some connection between freedom and the right to own the labor of our bodies and to some extent—the qualification is important—the right to own property, whether or not produced by our labor. More precisely, my contention is that a social order in which there exists a partitioned-off economic realm is necessary for political and social freedom, and that to date the only such social order has been that of capitalism.

Here we begin with the powerful fact that no noncapitalist country has attained the levels of political, civil, religious, and intellectual freedom found in all advanced capitalisms. To make the case differently, the state of explicit political liberty we loosely call "democracy" has so far appeared only in nations in which capitalism is the mode of economic organization. What is important, however, is the argument behind this connection. It is certainly not that the pursuit of capital breeds a liberty-loving frame of mind. It is rather that the presence of an economy within a polity gives an inestimable aid to freedom by permitting political dissidents to make their livings without interdiction by an all-powerful regime. Constitutional guarantees are no doubt the bedrock on which liberties of all sorts stand, but the presence of a private realm within an otherwise all-embracing state nonetheless provides the equivalent of a neutral Switzerland in which the enemies of the state can seek refuge.

It must be obvious that this refuge is far from perfect. The economy is often loath to accommodate individuals who are considered enemies of the social order: subversive intellectuals, radical politicians, and such. The availability of private employments serves only very imperfectly to allow dissenters to preach their unpopular views with impunity. Even more egregious is the blanket apology that this justification for property offers for the abuse of economic power or the vulgarization of acquisitiveness. Nor should it ever be forgotten that the espousal of democratic socialism, never mind theoretical communism, has often been considered a kind of *lèse-majesté*, thereby treating an economic preference as a political betrayal. Just the same, one cannot lose to sight the risk to freedom that exists in countries where no buffered territory called The Economy exists. Capitalism provides that Switzerland as part of its constitutive make-up.

III

The public and private realms of capitalism that establish the framework for its political life do not easily coexist, for they are motivated by different imperatives. We are by now familiar with the drive of accumulation that energizes the private realm. But from its earliest appearance the state has also had its own imperative—its *raison d'é-tat*—that has not only guided rulers and their entourages, but has exerted a magnetic field capable of capturing individuals of all social classes.

This political magnetism can be discovered to varying degrees in many institutional forms—ancient Greek city states, constitutional and absolute monarchies, democratic republics, totalitarian regimes. Behind these diverse political forms, however, we can discern a common appeal, analogous to the mobilizing power of capital in its capacity to marshall an entire citizenry. In the case of the state, however, the appeal is not that of achieving individual distinction through economic success but, quite the opposite, that of achieving distinction by merging individual selves into a collective whole. No doubt the attraction of this self-obliterating identity finds its roots in the buried fantasies of infantile existence, as does the self-aggrandizing appeal of the drive for wealth, although in the "political" case it is the identification of infant and parent, later socialized into family and tribal loyalties, that provides the root source of the phenomenon. Some such recourse to deep-seated human needs seems necessary, whether one merely seeks to explain why people line the street for a glimpse of a national leader, or why racial or religious identities are capable of wielding the immense destructive powers that threaten civilization in our time.

The glimpse of human nature reminds us again of the larger setting in which this study of capitalism must ultimately be placed. More immediately, it raises the question of how such differently constituted realms of authority make their mutual peace. The answer brings us back to operative characteristics of a capitalist order. For we have only to observe the interactions of the two realms at work to see that despite their fundamental difference, strong affinities bind each to the other. The realm of capital cannot perform its accumulative task without the complementary support of the state, as Adam Smith clearly perceived. On the other side of the coin, government is dependent on the healthy condition of the economy for the revenues it needs for its own goals, virtually all of which are expensive.

In this mutual dependency, the realm of capital has traditionally held the upper hand. To be sure, the state wields the stronger weapons—we commonly say that the power to tax is the power to destroy—but the ability to tax would be an empty privilege if the economy were not operating satisfactorily. Thus, in ordinary times the first concern of the state is to assist and support the accumulation of capital. Far from "crowding out" the private sector, the government makes way for it to move in. It is not out of weakness, but from considerations of its own interest that the business of government is business, as Calvin Coolidge put it succinctly.

By way of completing our overview of this normal congruence of interest, we should note that the relation between the realms has changed along with the changing technological and institutional texture of the system. In Smith's time, the role of the state was largely identified with aristocratic views and interests, and uncertain as to its appropriate role vis-à-vis the emerging market economy. To no small degree, *The Wealth of Nations* was a manual for government in its time. By mid-nineteenth century, government was everywhere openly associated with the promotion of bourgeois interests at home and abroad—Marx's *Capital* becomes its exposé. Today, the relation of polity and economy has changed again, this time with the state taking on functions needed to protect the economy from the increasingly threatening consequences to which an unregulated market could lead. These state interventions began with such now familiar problems as unemployment insurance and social security programs, and are today turning in the direction of the unfamiliar problem of shielding the economy against the incursions of global economic forces.

We shall shortly return to this last issue, but a final word seems necessary in this initial consideration of the interplay between the state and the economy. When national sovereignty is threatened, capital comes quickly to its aid. This is not from quite the same considerations that motivate the government to support enterprise. The public realm will certainly languish if the needs of the private realm are not met, but the existence of the private realm is not likely to be threatened if the public realm suffers political setbacks—the capitalist order has withstood many shifts of political fortune, including the coming to power of self-styled socialist parties. Indeed, after World Wars I and II it has even survived military defeats. Thus business rushes to the support of government more from motives of patriotism and possibly also profit, than in defense of political principles. Perhaps one can sum it up by saying that business stands behind government in emergencies and government stands behind business between emergencies.

IV

If that were all there were to the politics of capitalism, it would consist of little more than the mutual adjustment of these differing but not inconsistent goals. At its most difficult, it would raise problems of the kind foreshadowed in Smith's examples—problems arising from interventions of government that interfere with the adaptability and flexibility that are the economic achievements of a Society of Perfect Liberty, and from the corresponding tendency of business to seek political advantages that may diminish the potential energy of a competitive market system.

These are by no means minor conflicts of interest—one thinks of the bitter battle in the last quarter of the nineteenth century over curbing the behavior of big business, or more modern-day conflicts between government and business with respect to the choice between ecological considerations and profits. Nevertheless, these conflicts are no more than the everyday politics of any industrial system, not different in their origins or resolution from similar divergences of interest between planners and managers in the former Soviet Union. This is not the case with two other issues, both of which spring from the process to which we turn again and again as the wellspring of capitalist vitality—the expansion of capital. As we will see, however, they involve aspects, or consequences, of that drive that we have not heretofore considered at any length.

The first of these brings us to see capital accumulation itself from a different perspective than that to which we are accustomed. The perspective focuses on the geographic reach of the search for the resources, labor, and markets that make up the actualities of the capital-generating process. And as soon as we look with this question in mind, one realization springs to the fore. The economic reach of capital is immeasurably longer than the political reach of the national entities from which it emanates. The accumulation of capital takes place on an international—perhaps more accurately, a transnational—scale that lifts it "above" the nation-states in which it locates its operating units. Overarching these nation-states, the process of converting commodities into money, and money back into a larger value-sum of commodities, takes place like a great stream of economic traffic moving across a bridge supported on the piers of mines, plants, offices, and research centers located in various parts of the world.

The magnitude of this transnational stream has become enormous. According to a recent study of the United Nations' Center on Transnational Corporations, the combined sales of the 350 largest transnational corporations in 1985 amounted to almost one-third of the combined gross national products of all industrial countries and exceeded the aggregate GNPs of all the developing countries, including China.[28] This is tantamount to a world economy within a world economy. As such, it introduces a new strain on the endemic political problem of the relationship of capitalism's two realms. From their earliest days, all capitalist economies have taken advantage of differences in international costs—especially labor costs—as a primary source of capital: Keynes once estimated that the treasure brought back on Sir Francis Drake's *Golden Hind,* compounded at existing rates of

---

28. Gerard Piel, *Only One World,* New York, W. H. Freeman, 1992, p. 246.

interest, was equal to the entire wealth of pre–World War I Britain[29]; and the largest single source of capital accumulation in the modern world is that amassed by the petroleum industry, until twenty years ago, by buying oil in the underdeveloped world for a pittance.

International trade connections are not, however, the same as transnational ones. The latter do not merely involve the extraction of a commodity cheaply in one country and its sale in another, more developed one, but entail a network of production, research, and merchandising activities that are spread among many nations, some developed, some not. Thus the Chrysler Corporation, an "American" company, builds its most successful car in Canada; the "Japanese" Honda is produced in the United States; the Pepsi-Cola company makes its products in 500 plants located in 100 countries; the Phillips, Asea-Brown Boveri, and Electrolux companies, all of them members of the club of 350 multinationals, are in many ways too large to be contained in their "home" economies of the Netherlands, Switzerland, and Sweden.

What emerges in this increasingly globalized pattern of production is a challenge to the traditional relationship between the economy and the state. The globalized market system stretches beyond the political authority of any single government. Faced with a network of connections that escape their powers of surveillance or regulation, national governments have become increasingly unequal to providing the legal, monetary, or protective functions that are their contribution to a well-working economy.

29. John Maynard Keynes, *A Treatise on Money,* Vol. II, London, Macmillan, 1953, pp. 156–57.

Worse, the home nation finds itself with divided loyalties—on the one hand eager for "its" firms to maximize revenues, which are subject to national taxation; on the other, reluctant to see employment or research capabilities that it wants as part of its national economic strength located in a competitive national entity.

To date, this conflict of aims has usually been settled in favor of the transnational expansion of the firm, as the statistics of explosive growth indicate. What is uncertain is whether this movement can continue unimpeded. Just as the trillion-dollar-a-day market for foreign exchange effectively places the valuation of any nation's currency at the pleasure of "the market" rather than at the discretion of its monetary authorities, a similar unification of economic production would mean an unprecedented diminution in the capacity of any individual nation-state to seek an economic destiny that departed in any substantial measure from that of its political rivals. As many economists will point out, that may bring about an increase in the average level of "efficiency" among nations; but as these same economists must admit, it also means an unparalleled loss in the economic independence that some of them might wish to seek.

Thus the internationalization of economic life appears to be changing the relationship between the economy and the state. Over the course of history, the state, with its clumsy procedures, has been no match for the quick-moving forces of economic life. The economy has dominated the polity in capitalist history to an extent unimagined in previous regimes. Nonetheless, in our times we hardly need to be reminded of the latent powers that lie within the political realm. In ordinary times men will go to great lengths to make money, but they will rarely, if ever, die for it. In extraordinary times they will die in droves for their country, although they may ordinarily not be willing to lift a finger for it. Much depends, therefore, on whether the political strains of an ever more internationalized economy cross the line that divides ordinary from extraordinary times. If the line is not crossed, the globalization of economic life will make its peace in one way or another with the boundaries of political independence, and capitalism will continue under much the same general rules, despite changes that may considerably affect the respective rankings of its Center powers and their Peripheral dependencies. But if that line should be crossed, no such general expectation would be warranted. We would then witness an assertion of national identity in defiance of economic trends, very likely by the formation of semi-autarchic national groupings. The logic of economics, which has guided so much of modern history, will then be edged aside—although I am sure not displaced—by that of politics. And what is the logic of politics? One suspects it will have to be learned the hard way.

V

A second, no less far-reaching tension also brings into question the framework of the two realms. This is the relation between the economics of expansion and the domestic political peace of the system. We have already seen how the beginnings of the accumulation process brought disquiet to Elizabethan England through the enclosure of the commons. With growing intensity that disquiet persisted throughout the nineteenth century and a third of the way through the twentieth century. Save for a few placatory gestures, primary among them the introduction of the first social security legislation by Chancellor Otto Bismarck, the response of governments to this threat was expressed in repressive legislative and regulatory measures. To a great degree this was no doubt an expression of class hostility and fear, and to a lesser degree of indifference or inertia. But there is no doubt that a contributory element was the conviction that there was little that government could do to solve the problem of economic instability, except to allow the system to recover its "natural" vitality. Political intervention was not only contrary to the nature of things but useless to boot.

The 1930s changed all that, and the second half of the century has changed it again, to bring us to the economic impasse that is one of the marks of capitalism in our day. The initial change was brought on by the Great Depression that reduced gross national product in many countries by more than a third, and in some by as much as half; increased unemployment to 25 percent of the labor force in the United States; and shrank the volume of international trade for fifty-three consecutive months. Capitalism unquestionably then stood nearer to overthrow or collapse than at any time in Marx's life. Indeed, in Germany, Italy, and Spain, capitalism made way for a kind of bastard system that retained some of the drive for accumulation and some of the market mechanism, but that largely destroyed the partitioning of realms. The bastard system was called fascism, and the change in the relation of the realms consisted in the subordination of the economy to the state.

As we all know, the thirties were also the period in which capitalism underwent a profoundly important change in those countries where no such subordination took place. The change involved an expansion of the role of the public realm, but with a decisive difference. In the fascist states something like a seamless web of authority was once again established, whereas in the democratic nations the change took the form of a new "duty" added to those of Smith's original three.

The new duty was to strive for what was called "full employment." This was very different from a subordination of the private sector to the ambitions of the public sector, because the expanded role of the state stopped far short of permitting it to guide, much less take over, the activities of the private sector. Full employment meant only that economic growth would be pushed to its feasible limits. John Maynard Keynes, whose *General Theory of Employment, Interest, and Money,* published in 1936, was the Magna Carta of the change, did indeed foresee a "somewhat comprehensive socialisation" of investment as necessary to rescue capitalism from the danger of chronic unemployment, but this enlarged function of the state was rendered as apolitical as possible by Keynes's outspoken support of capitalism and his equally outspoken distaste for socialism. The structural change he urged was therefore intended only to supplement the accumulation activities of the private sector by assuring a sufficiently high level of national spending. Keynes did not even think of using the enlarged public component of that spending to provide public investment, such as infrastructure. He wrote, tongue only halfway in cheek, that if sensible public investment outlets were hard to find, it would serve the purpose just as well if the Treasury filled old bottles with bank notes, buried them in disused coal mines, and let out contracts to dig them up.[30]

What Keynesian economics provided was a rationale for using the public realm in a previously undreamt of way: as a fiscal agency of the capitalist order, charged, as a minimal responsibility, with the prevention of massive unemployment and, as a maximal one, with the attainment of full employment. There is no doubt that the first responsibility was discharged with success. In the United States the test did not take place in the 1930s, when government expenditure rose only modestly and unemployment accordingly remained at about 15 percent of the work force until 1941. It was the war that demonstrated irrefutably that unemployment could be eliminated by Keynesian public policy: by 1943 unemployment was down to 3 percent. And while the rationale of war could not be continued after 1945, the emerging political acceptance of the welfare state provided a new legitimation for enlarged public expenditure. Throughout Western capitalism, government spending of all kinds—social security, unemployment insurance, family allowances (except in the United States), as well as the more traditional purchases of public goods and services—rose from pre-

---

30. John Maynard Keynes, *The General Theory of Employment, Interest, and Money,* New York, Harcourt Brace, 1936, p. 129.

war levels of roughly a seventh of GNP to a third and even to a half. As a result, mass unemployment, the political as well as the economic scourge of the 1930s, disappeared as the central threat to capitalism.

The second responsibility—the provision of full employment—was, however, more problematic than the first, for a new challenge now emerged from the very success of the welfare state. The challenge lay in the effect of prolonged prosperity in strengthening the bargaining power of labor. With differences from one country to the next, the position of labor changed from that of a largely nonunionized, passive group, grateful for an offer of work and unable to make militant claims with respect to its rate of remuneration, to a well-organized, generally aggressive participant in wage negotiations. As the labor market hardened, all advanced countries began to feel a powerful pressure exerted by rising wages against the level of prices. By the end of the 1970s, the cost of living was rising five to ten times more rapidly than in the early 1960s. After 1973, when the oil cartel added "oil shock" to the "cost-push" of the labor market, half the Western capitalisms were experiencing double-digit inflation.[31] Meanwhile, the tying of many payments, from wages to Social Security, to the cost of living, removed the inflationary brake of contractually fixed income payments.

The advent of inflation, following the apparently effective conquest of depression, brought about the second sea change to the politics of capitalism. On the face of it, the change was a shift toward system-stabilizing, rather

31. John Cornwall, *The Theory of Economic Breakdown,* Cambridge, Mass., Basil Blackwell, 1990, p. 40.

than system-expanding policies. High interest rates, a bane of Keynesian economics because of their depressing effect on employment, became a widely used instrument of national policy precisely because a stagnant economy, with all its problems, developed less inflationary pressure than a booming one. A climax was reached in 1984 when short-term interest rates in the United States reached an unprecedented 20 percent as the result of a relentless, and eventually successful, campaign by the Federal Reserve to bring the United States' inflationary spiral under control. With this came the abandonment of full employment as the primary target of national economic policy. As inflation became the chief economic enemy, "acceptable"—that is, desired—levels of unemployment rose from the two to three percent levels advocated by United States administrations during the 1960s to five and six percent in the 1980s. A similar shift was openly expressed in the fiscal and monetary policies of all capitalist countries.

VI

What has been the ultimate impact of Keynesian economics on the politics of capitalism? The question really means: how successful has been the policy of government intervention in sustaining the vitality of the economic system?

The answer is not simple. Despite Keynes's own measured political views, his economics was at first regarded as a radical critique of capitalism because of its explicit doubts as to the self-sustaining capabilities of the unsupported private sector. But it is possible to see early Keynesianism in a different light, as a powerful force for enhancing the economic stability, and thereby moderating the political temper, of the system. As the postwar boom went on, it became ever more difficult to interest a relatively contented labor force in seeking far-reaching emendations in a social order that was working very well. Even in those nations, such as Sweden, where policies of substantial income distribution and social welfare were introduced, the aim of its "socialistic" measures was always to test the outer limits of liberal capitalism, not to cross over into the uncertain terrain of a revolutionary postcapitalist society. In the second phase of the postwar world, this conservative turn became even more apparent. As successful Keynesianism gave way to chronic and endemic inflation, the anti-inflation policy of governments bore down much more painfully on labor than on capital. Thus, despite its reputation, the effect of Keynesian economics both in its early and later forms seems to have strengthened the interests of capital rather than undermining them, and thereby to have served a conservative, not a radical, political end.

I said, however, that I do not think the political effect of Keynesianism is easy to assess. For if there is one conviction that is central to conservatism, it is that the system as a whole functions best when it is least constrained by government. What we find in both the heyday and the decline of Keynesianism is precisely the opposite of this. In the first period, government came to be viewed as responsible for growth; in the second, as responsible for stopping inflation. In both periods the common conviction—expressed in the language of action, not in the rhetoric of politics—was that government held the key to the economic future, and that a failure on its part would seriously damage the prospects of that future.

This is not old-fashioned conservatism. It is the expression of an often uncomfortable awareness that the economic order of the system is more integrally connected with, and more dependent on, the political order than used to be thought the case. What we see is the penetration of the economic processes of the system by its political realm, not driven by ideology but by necessity, not taking the lead in a conscious redesign of capitalism, but coming up from behind to shore up its means of securing its own future.

In my opinion no single issue will be more profoundly determinative of the future of the system than the relation of its two realms. I do not mean by this that there exists some "optimal" mix of public and private spheres. On the contrary, I am certain that the configuration will vary from country to country, depending on many elements, not least that of "national character." Some years ago the sociologist Seymour Martin Lipset compared two countries, similar in many respects, including a common challenge that had shaped the outlook of each. The two countries were Canada and the United States, and the challenge was that of settling a vast wilderness. Out of this common adventure two very different figures emerged as national heroes. For Canada, it was the Northwest Mounted Police. For the United States, it was the cowboy.[32] One would not expect two nations that have drawn such different meanings from similar historic experiences to resolve the problem of the two realms in the same way.

We will revert more than once to this vital issue. Perhaps, however, it would be well to conclude this chapter by recalling that the public-private relationship itself is not beyond change. The United States, today so fearful of considering the public sector as an active partner in the revitalization of capitalism, once turned with alacrity and trust to the government as the funding source for its early nineteenth-century network of canals, then for the financing of the massive Erie and, still more massive, Panama canals; for the underwriting of its transcontinental rail system, and much later of its Interstate Highway System; for the electrification of its rural areas; for its Tennessee Valley Authority and its Manhattan Project; for its moon landing; for its National Institutes of Health; and much more. Thus there is more than one national tradition on which we can draw. If I were to risk one prediction with respect to the future of American capitalism in the twenty-first century, it is that its success will hinge on the capacity to perceive the public sector, as did Adam Smith, in terms of an indispensible source of strength for a private economy, not as a wasteful drag on it.

---

32. Seymour Martin Lipset, *The First New Nation: The United States in Historical and Comparative Perspective,* New York, Basic Books, p. 251.

5

The Market
System

I

THESE DAYS WE tend to speak of capitalism as "the market system," especially when addressing people in those parts of the world where "capitalism" is still a suspect term, but the euphemism is unwise. For markets are a part of capitalism, but not the whole; and the discrepancy between the two is very great. We would have had no trouble explaining to the village elders of our first chapter what markets were, because they would likely be found in every village of their country. We had a great deal of difficulty telling them what a society would be like if markets embraced every aspect of economic life down to the very choice of tasks that each individual should perform, for such a "system" would be found nowhere in their country. And even such a system is only a part of capitalism. As the citizens of the former Soviet Union are discovering to their consternation, a market system means the end of the long lines for bread that were a curse of life in a society of centralized command, but it also means the introduction of a line that did not exist formerly—namely, standing in line at employment offices, looking for work.

Thus, capitalism is a much larger and more complex entity than the market system we use as its equivalent, and a market system is larger and more complex than the innumerable individual encounters between buyers and sellers that constitute its atomic structure. The market system is the principal means of binding and coordinating the whole, but markets are not the source of capitalism's energies nor of its distinctive bifurcation of authority. Markets are the conduits through which the energies of the system flow and the mechanism by which the private realm can organize its tasks without the direct intervention of the public realm. This suggests that our task in this chapter will be to separate the part from the whole, learning how this remarkable mechanism works, while holding in mind that the real object of our investigation is the fate of the social order within which the market exerts its powerful integrative and disintegrative forces.

These days one does not much hear about the Invisible Hand, Adam Smith's marvellous metaphor for the market system. The system is all too visible in the form of corporate maneuvers or garish advertising, but "the market" has attained a degree of admiration and respect that would certainly have pleased Smith. This is the direct consequence of the economic disaster that has befallen the Soviet Union. In the old USSR, almost the only goods whose supply matched the demand for them were the very special outputs of the ministries of defense. Ordinary goods, especially for consumers, did not fare so well. Russian consumers "shopped" by hearing rumors that shirts were available at the clothing outlet on Chekov Street, or that the state bakery on Tolstoi Prospekt had a supply of cakes. Consumers often discovered that the shirts lacked buttons or the cakes taste. Things were more serious when certain kinds of goods, such as hospital supplies, were in such short supply that hospital deaths rose alarmingly; or when spare parts were so difficult to procure that factories were forced to make their own; or when goods for export were so technologically obsolete they could only be shipped to subservient trading "partners." In the end, the Soviet economy fell apart for lack of micro-order.[33]

In light of Soviet experience—mirrored to a great degree by all East European nations, Maoist China, and Cuba—it is not surprising that the market today enjoys a near-worshipful reputation. There is today widespread agreement, including among most socialist economists, that whatever form advanced societies may take in the twenty-first century, a market system of some kind will constitute their principal means of coordination. That is a remarkable turnabout from the situation only a generation ago, when the majority of economists believed that the future of economic coordination lay in a diminution of the scope of the market, and an increase in some form of centralized planning. For reasons I will discuss presently, I believe that the pendulum will swing back toward an appreciation of planning, although never to the degree

33. For an excellent overview see Nicholai Shmelev and Vladimir Popov, *The Turning Point,* op. cit.

that was common not so very long ago.

All that, however, takes us into a consideration of problems that we cannot fully appraise until we have looked into a matter that has been alluded to, but not explained. It is how the market works. It is the answer to the uneasy disbelief of the village elders that a society run by self-interest could be counted on to provision its needs—a disbelief expressed more than once, I am certain, by many leaders of underdeveloped nations in their talks with officials of the International Monetary Fund and the World Bank. Until we can answer that question in our own minds, we cannot proceed to the larger task at hand.

II

An economist will tell us that markets introduce micro-order into a society. By micro-order they mean the equivalent of an Invisible Hand that leads men by the elbow to achieve social ends that were not part of their conscious intent. The economist's explanation begins, as did Smith's, from the assumption that a "maximizing" mind-set is a given of human nature. A question that immediately comes to mind is what mind-set would serve the same purpose in a society that was not a slave to acquisitiveness. For lacking such a peremptory inner directive, market systems will not work. The paradox of markets is not that they bring order out of a universe of individuals seeking only to "augment their fortunes," but that they will work only in such a universe. The problem in coordinating a society that does not cultivate an acquisitive mentality is that it lacks a force field that will exert a predictable effect on its members' behavior. That opens the difficult question of whether some force field other than acquisitiveness might serve as well, a matter we will look into in our final pages.

Meanwhile, I see no reason to doubt that there is acquisitiveness enough to drive the market system, evidenced by the seemingly insatiable appetite with which individuals endeavor to increase their personal capitals. This orientation now leads to three specific patterns of action that together produce the results that so baffled our village council. The first such pattern is that individuals will follow whatever feasible path best promotes their economic interest. This means that they will tend to seek out the best paying jobs for which they are suited, readily leaving one employer, and on occasion even one occupation or region, for another, if it pays better. The first function of a market system is thus to allocate labor to those tasks that society wants filled. Indeed, a market system cannot exist if there are barriers that prevent this self-motivated channeling of labor power, which is why one cannot have such a system in a society of slaves, serfs, or centrally allocated labor. The market is thereby linked to a Society of Perfect Liberty in more than a merely rhetorical way.

The second pattern affects the same channeling of effort with respect to the use that employers make of their capital. Also in pursuit of self-interest, they will increase the production of those goods and services for which demand is greatest and presumably profits highest, and reduce production where demand and profits are relatively low. In this way, as with labor, demand acts as a kind of magnet for supply, further assuring a match between the two.

These first two effects of a market system are simple to grasp. It is the third pattern that requires some thought. This is the internecine conflict that affects the activity on each side of the market, as competition develops among both suppliers and demanders. In the labor market, workers vie with one another to secure the better paying jobs. In the market for products, employers vie for shares of the public's purchasing power. The effect in all cases is to force prices of every kind, including wages and rates of profit, to the prevailing social level. The market system thereby becomes its own policing agency against the exactions of greed and the inequities of exploitation. Oddly enough, this self-policing process is also driven by self-interest, even when this involves reducing one's immediate gain. The supplier who will not lower a price that is out of line will be bypassed in favor of another; a buyer who will not meet the going market price will not be able to purchase what his competitor can.

I think I can sense murmurs with regard to this idyllic portrayal of the market, and I can promise a second look that will be less uncritically admiring. But understanding must come before criticism. Let me therefore add a few more words of explication, comparing the workings of a centrally planned and a market system.

Let us suppose that there is a shortage of some good in both societies, shoes for example. In a command society, shortages lead to lines that satisfy those who are at the head and disappoint those at the end. They may also lead to instructions from the consumer goods ministry to its footwear division to increase output. I say "may lead" because the process of changing schedules of output is fraught with difficulties in a bureaucratic system, where there is a powerful incentive to leave things be—laissez-faire is not a slogan of planned societies, but laissez-passer may be. During the 1930s there was a famous debate between the conservative economist Ludwig von Mises and the socialist economist Oskar Lange as to the prospects for a coherent system of central planning. Mises declared flatly that such a system was "impossible" because the planners could never amass the information that a market system continuously and effortlessly displayed in the price "signals" that told marketers what to do. Lange claimed that precisely the same information would be available in a planned system in the form of inventory levels, which would rise when supply exceeded demand and fall when demand exceeded supply. When inventories rose, planners would know that supplies had to be reduced, so they would lower prices paid to suppliers and raise them for consumers, thereby discouraging output. When inventories fell, planners would do the opposite—raising prices for suppliers, reducing them for consumers. Thus inventory levels would give the planners the exact same information that they would get from price signals in a market system.[34]

---

34. See Ludwig von Mises, "Economic Calculation in the Socialist Commonwealth," in *Collectivist Economic Planning,* ed. Friedrich von Hayek, London, Routledge & Sons, 1935, p. 105, and Oskar Lange and Fred Taylor, *On the Economic Theory of Socialism,* New York, McGraw-Hill, 1938, pp. 87–89.

History proved Mises to be devastatingly correct as to outcome, but, I think, not for the right reason. The enemy was not an absence of information—the staffs of the planning apparatus in the Soviet Union knew when shoes were in short supply or (more rarely) in surplus. What they lacked was the incentive to do anything about it. Self-interest counselled leaving things alone, not doing something. Hence bureaucratic inertia was the enemy— in the end, the mortal enemy—of the planning system. Ironically, Lange had sensed that this was the crux: *"The real danger of socialism,"* he wrote, in italics, *"is that of a bureaucratization of economic life."* But he took away the sting when he added, without italics, "Unfortunately, we do not see how the same, or even greater, danger can be averted under monopolistic capitalism."[35]

What Lange should have said was something else: the great source of disorder in command economies is the absence of a framework in which self-interest leads to socially useful action. With that in mind, let us now turn to the market economy, where we will suppose there is also a shortage of shoes. Here, shortages give rise to a series of stimuli that are lacking in a controlled system. Urgent telephone calls from shoe stores cause shoe manufacturers to raise production levels. In the same fashion, their own increased needs will lead to urgent telephone calls to leather manufacturers to increase shipments; and this in turn to further calls from leather manufacturers to buyers at cattle auctions.

From this flurry of activity, prices will rise: first at the

35. Lange and Taylor, ibid., pp. 109–10.

auction, then in the price of hides and leather, finally in shoes. As production flows increase, more labor will be needed, perhaps more machinery. The word gets out that the shoe industry is hiring at good wages. Shoes come back into stock, but they are more expensive than before. Consumers buy fewer pairs per year than they used to. Expansion in the shoe industry tapers off. The shoe shortage becomes a thing of the past. A new pattern of outputs, wages, and prices has brought about a stable situation in the shoe industry: telephone calls cease. Micro-order reigns supreme, although no one has done anything but follow the arrow of self-interest every step along the way.

III

It is important to bear in mind how a market system acts in theory, because most of the time it also works more or less that way in practice—if it did not, capitalism would long ago have collapsed. I say "most of the time" because markets are working even when we are wholly unaware of them—indeed, they are working at their best at those times. As long as markets provide coherence and order, we are quite unconscious of their presence, as we would be of a planning system if it too worked satisfactorily most of the time. I need hardly add that markets do not always behave in this orderly and invisible fashion. On the contrary, from time to time they work in highly disorderly and attention-attracting ways, for example, when the stock market crashes or the oil market runs amok.

What we need to understand now is why markets sometimes behave and sometimes do not.

Perhaps the oldest reason for market-caused problems lies in their changed characteristics in economies whose typical units of operation are no longer small, adaptable enterprises but large-scale, technologically "fixed" undertakings. The difference between the two can be described by the difference between a sand pile and a girdered structure. A pile of sand will hold its shape against many blows, but a structure of girders, although incomparably larger and stronger than the sand pile, can be toppled by the collapse of a single, strategically placed beam.

Capitalist societies start as sandpiles and end up as girdered structures. This is a direct outcome of the accumulation of capital—pin factories evolving over the course of time into industrial structures as large as small towns. Smith saw the competitive process as essentially one of securing and maintaining an equality of rewards within, or among, occupations and industries. That may have been an accurate perception in the time of pin manufactories but it was increasingly less so as the nineteenth century wore on, and the contending firms became large-scale textile mills and mechanized coal mines and then truly giant enterprises, such as railways. Such enterprises required expensive capital structures, and these structures in turn imposed large fixed costs, such as interest, which had to be met to remain solvent. The result was the rise of cutthroat competition that forced many weaker firms to the wall, where they were bought up cheaply by the firms that survived. Later, when cutthroat competition became too costly, the pressures of competition led instead to amalgamation by merger and trusts. In the United States, for example, most companies in 1865 were highly competitive, with no single company dominating any single field. By 1904 one or two giant firms controlled at least half the output in seventy-eight different industries.[36]

Thus the dynamics of competition itself became a major source of the transformation of an atomistic economy into one of structured strength and vulnerability. Alfred Chandler has shown how different national capitalisms have dealt with the ensuing threat to industrial stability—some working out uneasy arrangements of live and let live, others resorting to cartels, with varying degrees of tacit or explicit government agreement and approval.[37] In our own day, as we have seen, the problem has become still more complex insofar as the interconnectedness of the global economy widens the field of competition beyond national boundaries. The 350 corporations whose combined sales come to a third of the aggregate GNP of the industrial world are giant beams in the structure of world capitalism, and by that very fact, a new source of potential economic instability within individual national economies. Today there exists no effective means to protect production within a nation if the transnational structure should begin to shake. In this respect, we are in much the same condition of helplessness

36. R. Heilbroner and A. Singer, *The Economic Transformation of America: 1600 to the Present,* San Diego, Harcourt, Brace, Jovanovich, 1984, p. 203.

37. Alfred Chandler, *Scale and Scope: The Dynamics of Industrial Capitalism,* Cambridge, Mass., Harvard University Press, 1990.

with regard to maintaining individual flows of production that are threatened from abroad—automobiles as a case in point—as we were in the 1930s in maintaining our larger flows of output that were threatened from within.

Market disorders do not arise only from the increasingly girdered structure of production. They can also have a purely psychological basis. Suppose a shortage in the grain markets sends prices up. Ordinarily, higher prices would bring more grain into the market, perhaps from imports, while at the same time causing grain consumption to diminish. Micro-order will be easily restored. But now imagine that news of a potential drought reaches the floor of the grain exchange. Expectations about future grain prices soar. Thereupon, self-interest will no longer motivate supplies to sell grain at what were, only that morning, very favorable prices, but to hold back their supplies for the expected still higher prices to come. In the same fashion, buyers will not be deterred by today's high prices, but will try to fill their needs before things get worse. The result is exactly the opposite of the textbook case: the shortage will get worse, not better.

Whenever expectations point toward a worsening of existing conditions, market outcomes will not be equilibrating but disequilibrating. An initial mismatch of supply and demand will turn into a still worse one. Thus anything that affects mass psychology adversely can reverse the effect of self-interest from order-generating to disorder-generating actions. We faced precisely such disorders during the 1930s, when the bottom fell out of the grain markets as farmers rushed to sell and buyers stood around with their hands in their pockets; and something like the same process occurs during inflations, when sellers are in no haste to sell, and buyers can't wait to buy, thereby adding fuel to the inflationary fire.

This last takes us out of the context of a micro-disorder into the problems of economy-wide macro-disorder, which deserves a word by itself. For many years, economists believed that markets would regulate the overall level of employment as smoothly as they did that of the level of output of individual goods. If the employment level were too low, the market would cure the problem because wages would fall as unemployed workers competed to find jobs. As wages declined, employers would find it profitable to hire more help. Thus the market would cure an imbalance between the supply and demand for labor as effectively as for a single commodity. In much the same fashion, the market was also supposed to guide all saving into investment, the rate of interest serving the same function in the capital markets as the level of wages in the labor market.

But once again expectations can spoil this orderly process. When Keynes shocked the economic world of the 1930s by suggesting that the market mechanism would not necessarily drive the economy into full employment, his most telling argument was derived by applying to the determination of employment precisely the adverse effects that expectations can produce in determining the level of prices. Keynes asks us to suppose that employers see wages falling throughout the economy, and think about the effect of this on the demand for their own output. Will they hire more labor in the face of such an unpromising future? Will they risk putting funds into capital projects, no matter how low the cost of borrowing? The economy will still seek to balance the supply and demand for labor and for borrowed funds, but the point of equilibrium would not be the same as when expectations were buoyant.

Thus changing expectations change the outcome to which maximizing behavior will lead. This has unexpected consequences for those who see the market mechanism as providing an unchallengeable basis for capitalist operations. Critics of the market have long pointed out that a society whose economic activities are ruled by the market will be an attentive servant of the rich, but a deaf bystander to the poor. As a result, there is always a moral vulnerability to the micro-order that the market produces. We can now also see that there is a problem with respect to the macro-order that emerges from market considerations. Here the missing element is not morality—under certain kinds of expectations, the market may create more demand for employment than workers are willing to supply. There is, however, a vulnerability of another kind. In the case we have just mentioned, the market will produce a cost-push inflation, just as under the influence of the expectations about which Keynes wrote it will produce unemployment. Neither condition will be well suited to strong and steady growth. Both will, in fact, give rise to the sorts of difficulties we spoke about in the last chapter, in which the workings of the private realm generate difficulties that bring about a cry for public remedy.

IV

This brings us to what is perhaps the most pervasive and perplexing of all the influences that the market system brings to bear on capitalism. It is the effects that the market imposes all the time, whether it is working silently and well, or noisily and disruptively, effects of which we are sometimes acutely aware but more frequently quite ignorant.

In general, these market-related changes in our state of well-being are called "externalities." An example would be the higher laundry bills and health costs of people living in Pittsburgh before the pollution of the steel mills was brought under control. These costs are "external" in that, unlike the "internal" costs of the labor and raw materials that are paid by the mills, pollution costs are foisted on individuals who are external to the production process itself. Therefore steel producers have no incentive to cut down on pollution, insofar as they do not pay the laundry or health bills to which it gives rise.

As a result, the market mechanism does not accurately serve one of the purposes that it purports to fulfill— namely, presenting society with an accurate assessment of the relative costs of producing things. Suppose, for instance, that there are two ways of making steel, one of which is very clean but expensive, and the other dirty but cheap. Competition will push producers to choose the cheaper way, and an unsophisticated observer will say that the market has thereby helped society increase the efficiency of its operations. It could be, however, that if the laundry bills and health costs were added into the production cost, the cleaner process would turn out to be the cheaper. To the extent that this was the case, externalities will have steered society in the wrong direction, to a less rather than more efficient choice.

I said a moment ago that these were perhaps the most pervasive and perplexing influences that the market system imposes, and a moment's reflection will reveal why this is the case. There is virtually no act of production that does not have some external effects, sometimes good, sometimes bad. An individual builds a hideous house and depresses property values along his street. A business perfects a new product and opens new horizons for its users—transformational growth is largely a matter of favorable externalities. A nation enjoys strong economic growth and thereby hastens the advent of global warming.

To take into account all the external costs and benefits of production would be impossible. Yet, the failure to do so can seriously distort our assessment of the costs and benefits of production. The overcutting of forests, the overfishing of the seas, the overconsumption of gasoline are all instances of failures to include the full costs of producing various goods in their prices. Adam Smith was similarly concerned with an externality when he deplored the effects of subjecting working people to mind-numbing routines, and he would have been even more concerned had he taken account of the social costs that such an externality imposed. Thus externalities undermine a vaunted function of the market, which is to guide resources to their most rational use. Perhaps more tellingly, they reveal that the criterion of rationality is not the maximization of the public good, but of private profit; and that these two are by no means always the same, or nearly the same, because the market has no way of capturing and including those "side-effects" of production that escape its narrowly focused gaze.

There remains one further, as yet undiscussed impact of the market—an externality that affects our moral rather than our physical well-being. This is its effect on our culture. It is common to deplore the effect of the market mentality in promoting an ethic of selfishness, which is no doubt the case. But there are less obvious and therefore perhaps more insidious effects. The sociologist Michael Schudson has compared our exposure to smiling faces extolling the pleasures of automobiles and shampoos to that of the citizens of the former Soviet Union enthusing over coal and tractor production.[38] The difference, of course, is that Soviet propaganda was the product of a concerted and deliberate attempt to instill a kind of cultural patriotism, whereas capitalist advertising is only the product of an uncoordinated and chaotic effort to sell goods and services. Nonetheless, its effect is much the same. As the public voice of the private sector, advertising is the propaganda of a market system, just as propaganda is the advertising of a centralized one.

Schudson's assessment helps us become more aware of the wetness of the water in which we swim. Equally, per-

38. Michael Schudson, *Advertising: The Uneasy Persuasion,* New York, Basic Books, 1984, Ch. 4.

haps even more important are aspects of this cultural impact of which we are much less aware. One of these is the tendency to think of "production" only in terms of saleable goods, thereby rendering invisible such public goods as education or public health, of whose contribution to our well-being we are not constantly reminded. Even economists, who should know better, constantly apply such a double standard to the flows of national production. In the official accounts in which the nation's economic output is measured, we find private activities divided into two categories, "consumption" and "investment," of which the second is constantly praised as the locus of economic growth. In the same official accounts, however, there is no separation of "government expenditure" into categories of public consumption and public investment. Instead, all government spending is treated as if it were consumption, thereby treating the construction of a dam or a public research center as indistinguishable, in terms of its effect on growth, from the payment of congressional salaries or interest on the public debt. By way of turn around, the building of casinos in Atlantic City or Reno is deemed to be productivity enhancing, because the activity of building in the private sector is classified as "investment," without regard to what is being built.

This misperception reflects a market-oriented view of the economic process, in which all profit-making activity is considered also to be growth-producing, and in which all nonprofit-making activity is regarded as an essentially unproductive, although perhaps necessary, expenditure of effort. The result is a profoundly biased calculus of national performance or of suggestions for its improvement. The vocabulary in which we appraise the performance of the economy is already laden with the prerogatives of the very social order to which that presumably objective appraisal is applied. Thus, Smith anticipated Marx when he pointed out that "efficiency" blinds us to its cost in the degradation of the laborer, and the late E. F. Schumacher carried the point one step further when he observed that in "Buddhist" economics, labor would not be considered an "input" into the production process, but an "output" from it.[39]

V

To some, but not all of these market-related problems there are remedies. Regulation is one—government bans pesticides that are profitable to make but harmful to use. Taxes and subsidies can also be used to lessen the negative external effects of following the arrow of economic advantage by changing the direction in which the arrow points. In some cases, these measures can be extremely effective, as in the dramatic cleansing of Pittsburgh's air; in other cases, far less so, as in controlling automobile-caused pollution. In the same way, there are variations from nation to nation in dealing with the effects of market culture. Sweden has been vigilantly opposed to the side-effects of untrammeled commercialization on moral values; Japan indifferent to it; ourselves half-amused, half-appalled.

Thus, there is no single or simple way of describing

39. E.F. Schumacher, "Buddhist Economics," in *Small is Beautiful,* London, Bland & Briggs, 1973.

which externalities can be held in check and which cannot. Considerations of technology, political placement of affected industries, and of national sensitivity all play their roles in determining the degree to which we are victims of market dynamics as well as beneficiaries of them. From this point of view, externalities become another salient along which is waged the border warfare between the private and public realms. Insofar as industrial production is largely, although not entirely, carried on in the first realm, that is where externalities tend to originate; and insofar as their effects show up as costs imposed on citizens, their redress becomes a matter for action by the second. Here the sticking point seems to be whether control over a negative externality might prove too disruptive for the underlying economic process. It is a great deal easier to imagine the rigorous control over automotive emissions than a remedy for Smith's concern about the moral effects of the division of labor.

The question for the future then becomes our estimate of the extent to which market processes will threaten economic growth and stability and of the likelihood that the redress of market failures will lie within the political capabilities of a social order whose vitality lies in the accumulation of capital. As often before, little or nothing can be hazarded as to technological developments that may crucially affect externalities, for better or worse, or the political leverage of those who cause, or are affected by, market externalities, or with regard to the level of social concern with market failures. Nonetheless, two trends seem certain to add their pressures to the overall problem of coping with market dynamics. One of these, which we have mentioned more than once, is the growing tension between the imperatives of global economic integration and the counter-imperatives of its political compartmentalization. Although the outcome of this conflict remains uncertain, its very appearance raises to a new level of importance the contradictions between the dynamics of the market system and the consequences that emerge from them.

The second trend concerns the issue of global warming. The vast majority of nations today seek economic growth, whether for motives of profit, power, or social well-being. Economic growth hinges largely on industrialization, especially in the less developed parts of the globe where live five-sixths of the world's population who enjoy one-sixth of its wealth. Industrialization, in turn, results in the release of carbon dioxide from fuel, the gas rising into the atmosphere where it becomes part of an invisible windowpane that traps solar heat within the atmosphere. Without that windowpane, human population would perish of cold; but within the greenhouse itself, the addition of ever more carbon dioxide slowly raises the ambient temperature of the atmosphere.

Summing up the evidence, Paul Kennedy writes:

[T]he scientific consensus is that average global temperatures are between 0.3° C and 0.7° C warmer than they were a century ago. This is a modest rise, but the real concern is the rising pace of temperature increase in the *next* century, especially as world population and industrial activity grow. It is estimated that double the CO_2 levels will produce average temperature increases of between 1.5° C and 4.5° C by the middle of the twenty-first century. The difference between the "low" and the "high" figures is considerable, but even at a compromise figure of 2.5° C or 3.0° C, most scientists in this field hold that there would be serious consequences, [including] . . . rises in sea level, depleted agriculture, reduced water flows, increased health hazards (skin cancer, city smogs), more turbulent weather, social strains. . . . All suggest that both developed and developing nations have good reason to worry about global warming."[40]

Kennedy stresses the political disturbances that arise from the strains imposed by climatic change. From our perspective, the challenge goes to the viability of the capitalist order. The greenhouse effect places obvious barriers in the face of the accumulation process on which the system's life force depends. Perhaps even more directly, it questions the adequacy of the market to serve as the coordinating mechanism of the social order. A change in climatic conditions poses externalities of a gigantic order. Heat generated by industrial processes does not remain within the boundaries of the generating country, but spreads its effects everywhere. What will then be the attitude of the rich nations toward the industrialization of the poorer ones? What will be the attitude of the poorer nations toward the rich countries whose industrial production, even if stabilized, continues to account for the vast preponderance of all carbon emissions? The mechanism of resolution will have to be political, perhaps military—where, we should remember, all the trumps are not in the hands of the West. The prospect adds one last, perhaps most powerful reason to anticipate that the mar-

40. Paul Kennedy, *Preparing for the Twenty-First Century,* New York, Random House, 1993, pp. 105, 111. See also pp. 43–44 for the statement above as to the distribution of world population and wealth.

ket mechanism in the twenty-first century will surely be supplemented, and in some areas supplanted, by planning of one kind or another, not only within individual capitalist nations, but over them. Or perhaps, given the failure to find any such means of imposing transnational economic order to date, we should rephrase the conclusion to read that the prospect adds one last, perhaps most powerful reason to anticipate that unless the market mechanism in the twenty-first century is supplemented, and in some cases supplanted, by planning of one kind or another, we will find ourselves once again punished for not learning history's lessons.

6

Scenarios for the Future

I

I SAID AT the outset that I would not be so
foolhardy as to risk a grand prediction about
the future. That does not mean that I have condemned
myself to silence with regard to the prospects for the society in which our children and our children's children will
live. If one cannot speak of twenty-first century capitalism with the clarity and scientific certitude that the word
prediction conveys, we can nonetheless think about it in
terms of the scenarios by which the great economists
have projected the long-term trajectory of the system.

Scenario is a dramatic term. It implies that the future
has a developmental, rather than adventitious character—that it does not arrive from unknowable or unforeseeable causes, but as the unfolding of tendencies already
present in the structure and motivations of society. Thus,
for all their drama-like aspects, scenarios have the properties of exercises in logical analysis—indeed, their often
tragic characteristics derive from precisely this sense of

an impersonal force underlying and impelling the course of events. Scenarios thus project the powerful message that the economic future hinges primarily on the "workings" of a system, not on the assertion of age-old traditions or political command. From this point of view, the fact that predictions are unreliable becomes of less importance than that there exists the possibility of such a mode of inquiry in the first place. Economics will not allow us to foresee the fate of twenty-first century capitalism, but no appraisal of that fate can ignore the economic forces that will be instrumental in bringing it about.

Scenarios are a dramatic term for another reason, as well. It is that they combine powerful analytic frameworks with highly personal "visions" concerning the motives and the capabilities of the actors within those frameworks.[41] The visionary aspect arises from a growing recognition that however objective and logical analysis may be, it begins, as we have seen, from "facts" and descriptive observations already imbued with evaluative judgments. Such seemingly neutral words as *labor, capital,* and *government* have for all of us moral and political connotations of which we are generally less than fully aware, but which enter nonetheless into the roles they play in our presumably neutral analyses. Scenarios thus become vehicles for the expression of moral and political orientations, as well as exercises for the exploration of impersonal processes. This is both a deplorable weakness and an inescapable property of social inquiry. The pres-

---

41. See my "Analysis and Vision in the History of Modern Economic Thought," *Journal of Economic Literature,* Sept. 1990, pp. 1097–1114.

ence of values endows the exercise of analysis with an historical significance that it would otherwise lack. It thereby serves a vital existential purpose—to give answers to a question that would otherwise go unanswered: *What is the meaning of our historical plight?* We can accept many answers to this ancient inquiry, including tragic answers, but there is one response that would be unendurable. It is silence. Scenarios fill that void with respect to the future.

What do the scenarios of the past contribute to our construals of the future? One aspect strikes us immediately. Almost all are gloomy with respect to the long-term future of capitalism. As we shall immediately see, they are gloomy for very different reasons, but their common conclusion suggests that something is to be learned from examining their findings.

I suggest that we begin with a scenario that is already quite familiar to us. It is Adam Smith's expectations with regard to the Society of Perfect Liberty. As we have seen, Smith envisaged that society as bringing about a general increase in well-being for everyone, but he also anticipated that after a time it would accumulate "[the] full complement of riches" to which it was entitled by virtue of its resources and geographic placement. At this point accumulation would stop, and growth with it. The long upward gradient would thereupon turn downward, as a growing population divided up an output that had ceased to grow.

No doubt Smith's expectation was located as indefinitely in the future as is our own placement of the advent of a serious ecological barrier to growth. With all this qualification, his analysis of growth prospects is nonetheless ultimately pessimistic. To this he adds a "visionary" element—the apparent passivity with which the laboring class accepts the decline in its material fortunes. There is not the slightest hint of working-class resistance, much less revolt, in *The Wealth of Nations,* although Smith's analysis foredooms the laboring class to a decline in living standards to the barest subsistence. Perhaps this is the consequence of the moral deterioration that Smith also expects from the division of labor. Perhaps it was his expression of the widespread attitude of hopelessness with which all Enlightenment *philosophes* regarded the lower orders. In any event, in Smith's scenario the working class was destined to suffer immediate social decay as well as long-run economic decline. I do not exaggerate: "all the nobler parts of the human character may be in great measure obliterated and extinguished in the great body of the people."[42] Contrary to his popular reputation as the tutelary figure of capitalism, Smith is, of all economists, probably the least sanguine as to its long-run fate.

Marx, by way of contrast, is optimistic—not about capitalism, to be sure, but about the social order to which it will give birth. Surprisingly, the analytic element of his scenario resembles that of Smith's in many ways. Like his great predecessor, Marx's analysis traces out the consequences of an acquisitive drive in a competitive environment. Its conclusion differs from Smith's because Marx

---

42. Smith, *Wealth of Nations,* op. cit., p. 736.

replaces the manufactory with the much larger machino-factory, with the result that the expansion process becomes turbulent and disruptive rather than smooth and regulative, and its live-and-let-live masters are forced to become mutually destructive capitalists. Hence Marx's upward trajectory, quite unlike Smith's, is continually interrupted by periods of crisis and restructuring—it is the dynamics of a girdered not a sandpile economy.

Yet this dramatic difference, which stems from contrasting perceptions of technology, is not in itself sufficient to account for the contrast of the Marxian scenario with that of Smith's. What is ultimately decisive in this regard is Marx's vision of the working class as the agent of its own future liberation. Smith's uncomprehending laboring class is replaced by Marx's slowly awakening proletariat. Thus the Marxian scenario presents a different outlook from that of Smith's—not the historic rise and fall of societies, reminiscent of eighteenth-century views of the transient glories of Greece and Rome, but a directional process in which capitalism disappears before the advent of its successor, socialism.

Two other major scenarists also expect a troubled future for capitalism, once again for different reasons and with different outcomes. John Maynard Keynes is today regarded as a prophet of capitalist decline, but that fails to do justice to the complexity of his scenario. If Keynes was an analytical pessimist, he was a visionary optimist. He was pessimistic because his analysis of the workings of the market led to the disconcerting conclusion that a market-driven society could settle into a position of lasting underemployment. Very much like Smith, incidentally, that pessimism reflected a static view of technological possibilities. It is doubtful whether the *General Theory* would have manifested its discouraged tone had it been written in the postwar era of transformational change that Keynes did not live to see.

Keynes's pessimistic analysis was, however, balanced by an unexpectedly sanguine assessment of capitalist political possibilities. His vision inclined neither to Smith's despairing assessment of the laboring class, nor Marx's buoyant assessment of its revolutionary potential. Thus it was possible for Keynes to envisage with equanimity not only "the somewhat comprehensive" socialization of investment as the most feasible means of approaching full employment, but also the "euthanasia of the rentier,"[43] which is to say, the effective disempowerment of the monied classes. Yet, all the while, Keynes shrugged his shoulders at the idea of socialism, for which he entertained, at best, a kind of tolerant skepticism. His vision was therefore one of a stable and adaptive polity redressing the failures of an often ill-working economy, a position he described as "moderately conservative," although that was hardly the way most conservatives would have described it.

The great scenarists would not be complete without the inclusion of Joseph Schumpeter. He is at once an analytical optimist and a visionary pessimist. "Can capitalism survive?" he asks early in his magisterial *Capitalism, Socialism, and Democracy,* published in 1942. His answer is unequivocal: "No. I do not think it can."[44] The

43. John Maynard Keynes, *General Theory,* op. cit., pp. 376, 377, 378.
44. Joseph A. Schumpeter, *Capitalism, Socialism and Democracy,* New York, Harper & Bros., 1942, p. 163.

reason, however, is not that of Smith, Marx, or Keynes. Schumpeter introduces a new and much more dynamic element into the accumulation process: Marx's ruthless destruction of old capitals by competition is replaced by a "perennial gale of creative destruction" as entrepreneurs create and exploit previously nonexisting fields. Starting from such assumptions, Schumpeter therefore scoffs at the idea that the investment frontier can ever be fully occupied. Technological possibilities, he writes, are an "uncharted sea"; the airplane will be for the future what the conquest of India was for the past. Indeed, he concludes: "There are no *purely economic* reasons why capitalism should not have another successful run," at least in the short run—which, he has previously informed us in passing, is a century.[45]

Why, then, does Schumpeter expect the demise of capitalism? It is because he perceives the matter-of-fact, unsentimental point of view produced by capitalism as corrosive of the values on which the social order feeds. "Capitalism," he writes, "creates a rational frame of mind which, having destroyed the moral authority of so many other institutions, in the end turns against its own: the bourgeois finds to his amazement that the rationalist attitude does not stop at the credentials of kings and popes, but goes on to attack private property and the whole scheme of bourgeois values."[46] The end comes as the entrepreneurs who embody the élan of the system settle down for a secure existence as socialist managers.

Once more, vision rather than analysis sets the stage for this astonishing "prediction." In Schumpeter's view,

45. Ibid., pp. 84, 118, and 163, n. 7.
46. Ibid., p. 143.

entrepreneurs are members of elite groups that rise to the top in all societies: socialist government will assuredly make use of their "supernormal quality." On the other hand, workers, and the middle and the lower orders generally are creatures of habit and routine who will not even notice the difference in the transition from capitalism to socialism—"a family likeness" will make the latter much more like capitalism than different from it. Will this bourgeois, managerial, presumably democratic socialism work? Schumpeter has no hesitation: "Of course it will." He is as apodictic in declaring that socialism will succeed as in previously declaring that capitalism will fail. Indeed, he goes on to say that there is every reason to believe that the morale of socialism may be higher than that of capitalism, and that doubts about planning will come to look as nearsighted as those expressed by Smith about the future of joint-stock corporations.[47]

II

How can such mutually inconsistent, often historically disconfirmed expositions be of use in thinking about the prospect ahead? One possible answer suggests itself immediately: it is that none of our philosophers, not even Smith or Schumpeter, who are surely partisans of the capitalist order, project a long successful run for it.

Alfred Marshall, the great Victorian economist, ends his troubled and compassionate study with the hope that

47. Ibid., pp. 196, 198, 203, 204, 211.

"economic chivalry" will carry the day, but warns against "the hasty adoption of [methods progress] . . . which . . . while quickly effecting a little good, sow the seeds of widespread and lasting decay." Friedrich Hayek, who believes that capitalism is necessary to prevent mass poverty and death, nevertheless inveighs against the "fatal conceit" that humankind can shape its social environment as it pleases.[48] But why should the inhabitants of Marshall's text feel in the slightest tempted to undertake shortsighted solutions, and why should the denizens of Hayek's sober pages flirt with disaster if capitalism is, indeed, the only hope of civilization? These questions hang in the air, unanswered.

Why can we not find any major figure in the history of economic thought who projects an optimistic future? I think we can give one obvious and one somewhat suppositious reason for this widespread mood of apprehension. The obvious answer derives from the analytics of the problem. It lies in the sheer difficulty of successfully maintaining capitalist macro- and micro-order in the face of the range of self-generated problems that range across the three constitutive aspects of the system. Many economists fasten on the problems of maintaining the momentum of capital accumulation—Smith, Marx, Keynes as exemplars of a widely shared sense of impending saturation of demand and failure of purchasing power. Frictions between the public and private sectors are another focus for misgivings, whether these take the form of

---

48. Alfred Marshall, *Principles of Economics,* London, Macmillan, 1936, pp. 721–22; Friedrich Hayek, *The Fatal Conceit,* Chicago, University of Chicago Press, 1988, p. 27.

doubts that government can intervene to rescue capitalism from its ills because government cannot rise above narrowly conceived class interests, or the quite different doubts that capitalism's vigor can withstand the relentless expansion of the government as would-be regulator of the system: Marx represents the first view; many conservative economists the second. Not surprisingly, market dysfunctions are a third center for pessimistic analysis. We have seen the damage that can ensue from externalities, from self-aggravating expectations, and other market failures. I repeat again that the threat of ecological disaster is rooted in the inability of the market mechanism to resolve the global problem of pollution.

This by no means exhausts the specific reasons for economic pessimism. One can find scenarios in which the source of difficulty is located in the outlook for investment and for technology; in the unequal distribution of incomes; the volatility of credit; the tendency toward monopoly; the technological displacement of labor; the inflationary tendencies of a successful economy and the depressive tendencies of an unsuccessful one. What would be impossible to find are scenarios in which hitchless growth and adaptive survival carry the day. In the end, capitalism's uniqueness in history lies in its continuously self-generated change, but it is this very dynamism that is the system's chief enemy. The theme that runs like a basso ostinato through the overwhelming preponderance of scenarios is that the system will sooner or later give rise to unmanageable problems, and will have to make way for a successor.

I shall come back to that central finding, but I must next surface a more contentious explanation for this shared apprehension. It is rooted in what I believe to be a widespread sense of disquiet with regard to the moral basis of capitalism. Once again, Adam Smith surprises us by having recognized the underlying problem. He is writing here about the determination of the wages of labor:

. . . [T]he common wages of labour depend everywhere upon the contract usually made between two parties, whose interests are by no means the same. The workmen desire to get as much, the master to give as little as possible. . . . It is not, however, difficult to foresee which of the two parties must, upon all ordinary occasions, have the advantage in the dispute. . . . In all such disputes the masters can hold out much longer. Many workmen could not subsist a week, few could subsist a month, and scarce any a year without employment. In the long run the workman may be as necessary to his master as his master is to him, but the necessity is not so immediate.[49]

This is, needless to say, before the advent of unemployment compensation, industrial trade unions, and the welfare state, which have considerably redressed the inequality between labor and capital in the advanced industrial nations. Yet, Smith has his finger on a crucial point. In a market society where employers and workers enjoyed full equality of bargaining power, there could be no systematic favoring of one side over the other. In such a society it is difficult to see why some should agree to work for others, insofar as an equality of bargaining power pre-

49. Smith, *Wealth,* op. cit., Vol. I, Ch. 8. I have considerably condensed the original.

sumes that they would begin with equal amounts of resources. But even assuming that some would decide freely to become workers, why should their employers have left a surplus of revenues—profit—over what they paid out for in wages? Why would not employers, too, be paid wages, perhaps somewhat higher than those who worked with—surely not "for"—them, or why would not profits, if there were any, be divided proportionally among all?

It is Marx who places this question at the very center of his investigation into capitalism. I will not retrace his explanation of the manner in which the employer-labor bargain is resolved in such a way that all profits go to the employer. For our purposes, Marx's demonstration is interesting because it explains how this manifestly unequal relationship is made to appear entirely compatible with the idea of a system that eschews coercion. In a crucial application of the distorted perceptions imposed by a market system, Marx explains how the exploitation of labor becomes invisible because its rules of "free contract" hide Smith's distinction between those who can wait and those who cannot.

Marx is not an economist whose writings are on the standard reading lists for economics students, save perhaps for the *Manifesto,* read more often than not to point out its fatal over-optimism. But the issue he raises has stuck in the craw of economists. Endless pages have been devoted to demonstrating that workers would not be exploited in a "perfect" market where all the factors of production were paid the full value of their respective contributions to output. The answer in all cases tells us that profits are only the name for the return paid to capital—that is, the remuneration for the contribution that capital makes to production, exactly analogous to the payment called wages made for the similar contribution of labor. That which is left unaddressed is the nature of this return to the capital—let us picture it as picks and shovels—wielded by labor. Since picks and shovels do not have bank accounts, one might expect that their paychecks would be turned over to the factors of production who made them. But no, the earnings of capital are not paid to those who use it, or to those who made it, but to those who own it.

This poses a serious problem for those who wish to justify the moral basis of income distribution under capitalism. One might claim that the inequalities inherent in the private ownership of the means of production can be made morally acceptable by the need to maintain social order. That is in fact the position maintained by Adam Smith: "The peace and order of society," he writes in *The Theory of Moral Sentiments,* "is of more importance than even the relief of the miserable. . . . Nature has wisely judged that the distinction of ranks, the peace and order of society, would rest more securely upon the plain and palpable difference of birth and fortune, than upon the invisible and often uncertain difference of wisdom and virtue."[50]

This explicit acquiescence before the realities of the human social condition is not, however, an explanatory recourse to which many economists are willing to repair.

---

50. Smith, *The Theory of Moral Sentiments,* op. cit., Pt. IV, Sect. II, Ch. 1.

An exception is John Stuart Mill who defends inequalities of which he disapproves, writing: "While minds are coarse, they require coarse stimuli, and let them have them."[51] In general, the moral problems of the private ownership of the means of production are tactfully passed over. One does not read of the rationale that would convince Gai that one of his fellow-hunters should own all the bows and arrows, paying his !Kung brethren a share of the gemsbok agreed on before the hunt in exchange for owning the kill after it was brought down. Let me therefore advance a heretical suggestion. It is that the pessimistic consensus with respect to the long-term prospects for capitalism expresses moral misgivings among those who professionally seek to justify the social order in which they live. The problematic outlook they foresee for capitalism may not arise from bad conscience alone, but I suspect that bad conscience powerfully reinforces it.

III

It is time to turn to possibilities for twenty-first century capitalism. I shall begin with the problems of capitalist accumulation. We already know that we cannot make a plausible projection for the pace, steadiness, and volume of growth over the coming century. Capitalism is a system organized to search for, and to seize on, whatever technological and organizational changes offer profitable

---

51. *The Collected Works of John Stuart Mill,* Vol. III, Toronto, University of Toronto Press, 1981, p. 754.

chances for expansion, but it is not a system that has any way of assuring that these changes will arrive with the regularity and stimulative force required of them. I would think, therefore, that the most plausible scenario for its future is one in which the drive for accumulation will encounter the same successes and failures as in the past.

This is in itself neither an optimistic nor a pessimistic prospect. It is, rather, something much more difficult to accept: an inscrutable prospect. Hence, vision will assuredly enter into the picture, asserting either that the system will grow adequately, as it has, all things considered, for 150 years; or that it will encounter increasingly difficult obstacles, similar to its near-fatal collapse in the 1930s and its lackluster performance in recent years.

There is, however, another possibility—a response to the challenge of growth whose feasibility hinges on the second of capitalism's structural elements, its bifurcation of realms. The possibility is that capitalism may attempt to assure its required expansion by using public investment to provide whatever transformational impetus is lacking from the private sector. As the United States has learned to its distress, and as Europe and Japan have learned to their advantage, investments in public capital, from high-speed transportation to top-quality education, can make enormous contributions to productivity. Utilized as a deliberate agency for sustaining growth, investment in infrastructure might become the twenty-first century's solution to the problem of achieving and sustaining adequate growth, especially in the United States which has fallen so far behind in this regard.

There are, to be sure, very substantial problems to be overcome before this course could be tried. Again referring to the United States, the least formidable of them is the deficit, which is understood to be a crippling waste of public saving. I say this is the least formidable of our problems because it has a relatively easy resolution: to separate government expenditures for growth-promoting purposes from those for normal operating purposes. Government expenditures for its normal responsibilities, such as Social Security, health programs, defense expenditure, and the like, would then normally be covered by tax revenues, exactly as corporate operating expenses are normally covered by sales revenues. At the same time, government spending for growth purposes, such as infrastructure, would normally be financed by borrowing, as are investment outlays for business. Capital budgeting, which, incidentally, is used by every Western nation save our own, does not assure that government borrowing will be put to wise purposes. Rather, it exists to remind us that there are such purposes, and that deficits are not wasteful, but useful, when used for them.

As I have said, however, that is only the first hurdle in the way of utilizing the public sector to provide adequate growth. Two additional hurdles must be taken, each of them more difficult than the first. One of these is to raise our level of taxation. A strong and pace-setting public sector would require a much higher level of normal, non-investment expenditure for the care and maintenance of the national well-being than is possible with the starved revenues of our present tax system. According to a recent study, tax revenues as a percentage of gross national product in the OECD (advanced industrial) nations exceed those in the United States by a third. Only those of Japan are lower, and Japanese defense expenditures are less than one-sixth of ours. If we brought our tax revenues up to OECD proportions, we would increase federal tax income by at least $300 billion a year. If we added to that the borrowing that would be justified by a ten-year $1 trillion infrastructure program, such as that recommended by financier Felix Rohatyn, we would have a *masse de maneuvre* capable of imparting a substantial thrust to the economy.[52]

It remains to be added that the attainment of such a level of taxation would probably also require the adoption of a European mode of taxation. It is the curious fact that the United States raises a larger percentage of its revenues from direct income taxes than do the OECD nations—approximately 35 percent against an OECD average of 27 percent—and a much lower percentage of revenues by value-added or sales taxes—17 percent, as against 29 percent abroad. It is, in fact, likely that the American tax phobia results from this heavy reliance on income taxes, which are preferred by many economists because of their greater fairness, but detested by most taxpayers, who perceive them to be a kind of expropriation.[53]

---

52. For U.S. and OECD revenues and expenditures, see Louis A. Ferleger and Jay R. Mandel, *No Gain, No Pain,* New York, Twentieth Century Fund, 1993, Table 1. The Rohatyn proposal appeared in "What the Government Should Do,"*New York Review of Books,* June 25, 1992.

53. For comparative reliance on income and sales taxes, and the popular evaluation of different kinds of taxes, see Ferleger and Mandel, Ibid., Tables 6 and 7.

Unhappily, this is still not quite an end to the problem. There remains a difficulty of which we have already caught a glimpse—namely, coping with the inflationary pressures that can be expected to emerge from such a boom. Indeed, to the extent that a public expenditure program achieves its purposes, employment will tighten and wage rates will rise, setting into motion the kind of wage-price spiral that has been a plague for all late twentieth-century capitalisms.

Unlike the case with deficits, moreover, there is no means of dealing with these pressures by a mere change in our methods of keeping the national accounts. What is needed is a change in national institutions to prevent wage increases from running ahead of productivity growth, so that, speaking broadly, any increase in total wage payments will be matched by increases in output, thereby holding price rises to a minimum.

There are two ways in which this might be attained. One would be the creation of a kind of social contract among labor, management, and government along the general lines that have appeared in Germany. Labor unions are given a seat on corporate boards, with a voice in matters of labor policy, in exchange for an agreement to keep wage demands within noninflationary bounds. Management agrees to abstain from union-bashing tactics, in exchange for an agreement from its unions not to interfere in the efficient deployment of its work force. And government stands behind and makes effective the larger understanding by providing strong programs of unemployment insurance and retraining for labor, and a general support for corporate efforts to maintain their global market shares.

There is, of course, no guarantee that such arrangements would prove to be durable and effective. Hence there must also be a second line of defense against inflationary pressure. Insofar as voluntary agreements have been ruled out, this leaves only involuntary agreements, namely anti-inflationary tax programs. Despite the unpopularity of income taxes, inflationary tendencies can probably best be held in check by applying an inflation-geared tax against all income payments, dividends and interest payments as well as wages and salaries above a social minimum; or if that proves too much for the public to accept, an anti-inflationary boost in the national sales or value-added tax.

One has only to voice such proposals to be certain of facing a storm of protest. I will not attempt to head off this storm, but rather, use it to move our attention from the general problem of achieving growth to that of achieving social and political accord. This brings us again to the crucial structural characteristics of capitalism—its bifurcation into an economy and a state.

Once more I take my argument from a point of agreement in the scenarios of the great economists. For their scenarios share a common diagnosis beneath the variety of difficulties they perceive in the path of capitalist development. It is that the problems that threaten capitalism arise from its own dynamics, from problems generated within the private sector, not the public. The saturation of demand and the degradation of the labor force that are the great difficulties of Smith's conception; the crises and contradictions of Marx's model; the inability to reach full employment that Keynes selected as the great flaw; the cultural erosion of Schumpeter's scenario—these are all failures that are produced by the workings of the private realm, not of the public.

Inflation is a case in point. The inflationary pressures that would arise from a publicly launched boom have nothing to do with its government sponsorship. Precisely the same pressures will emerge if the private sector, quite on its own, discovers the ingredients of a transformational change. The fact to be faced is that under the conditions of late twentieth-century capitalism—and one suspects even more so in the twenty-first century—inflationary pressures lie at all times close to the surface and will have to be held in check, if not by a social contract then by some form of anti-inflation tax. Perhaps some more effective scheme can be realized, but its agent must be the government.

This raises again the issue of the politicization of capitalism: What solutions, what countermeasures can be brought to bear on the problems that arise from the private sector? Given the diagnosis, there can be only one answer—they must be solutions and countermeasures that arise from the public sector. From this it follows that the prospects for twenty-first century capitalisms—here I stress the plural—will depend, in the first place, on the success with which they can marshall and apply the forces of government to deal with those of their economies. The fundamental properties and problems of capitalism may be the same everywhere, but its governmental capability is not. Japanese capitalism, like Italian capitalism, is driven to amass capital, is both coordinated and destabilized by market forces, and is bifurcated into two realms; but the two capitalisms do not exercise public control over, do not provide public encouragement to, and do not supply public guidance for the performances of their economies with equal effectiveness. Everywhere national culture puts its stamp on the interaction of economic and political life. There is, if we recall, capitalism in the land of the Northwest Mounted Police and capitalism in the land of the cowboy.

Here, of course, we move from analysis, frail though it may be, to unsupported vision. What are likely to be the characteristics of a capitalism capable of mounting a public investment program if none emerges spontaneously from its private sector, of working out a viable social contract, and of imposing whatever anti-inflation taxes may be necessary? If I were to hazard such a description it would feature a strong tradition of pragmatic government and public cohesion, a well-developed civil service, and responsible national organizations of both labor and management. No doubt the institutional arrangements would vary from one such nation to the next, but like the more adaptive states of seventeenth-century Europe, I would think that some of these capitalisms could survive and even flourish for a long time. Again like seventeenth-century Europe, I would also think that unadaptive capitalisms, with restive and ideologically charged political traditions, weak structures of public administration, and nonorganized union and corporate sectors would almost certainly not fare well. Where the United States lies on such a scale, or where it might lie with adroit political guidance, I leave to my readers to decide for themselves.

Thus vision enters irrepressibly and naturally along with analysis. The exploration of the past and present orients us to the future, but what we see there depends to a very large degree on what we seek. That disconcerting and discomfitting conclusion frames my final responsibility. It is to make clear my own vision, insofar as I am aware of it. I shall do so by returning to our starting point—Kliuchevsky's terrible warning that history teaches no lessons but punishes severely if we do not learn them. It is time to ask what may be learned from the stylized history of capitalism, past, present, and possible that I have attempted to construct, and to speak directly to the questions I put at the outset: What is left of the idea of progress in human affairs? Does some form of socialism still lie after capitalism? Is human nature at the root of our problems?

7

History's Lessons

I

I BEGIN WITH the idea of progress, clearly en-
tangled in any attempt to speak of twenty-
first century capitalism against the backdrop of violence
and discordancy of which I spoke in my Introduction,
many pages back.

Since the early nineteenth century, progress has been
perceived as the movement of Western society "leftward" along an imaginary line that began in the feudal
past, ran through Early Middle and Late Capitalism, and
ended—or at least pointed toward—the dimly perceived
social formation called Socialism, and far beyond that,
Communism. By "leftward" I mean a direction of social
change whose prime mover was the emerging economic
dynamic within social life. In the opinion of almost every
historian, this slow, often interrupted, but persistent
movement was intimately connected with the idea of
progress. It is that view that now stands at bay.

The movement was deemed to be an expression of

progress for several reasons. The first was that the changing configuration of society was clearly the product of impersonal forces, which is the aspect that human behavior takes on when it responds to stimuli in predictable fashion. The stimuli themselves also appeared to be impersonal insofar as they too were composed of predictable behavioral tendencies, rather than the edicts of powerful personages, the outcomes of military adventures, and the like. Thus the nineteenth and twentieth centuries gave us the extraordinary spectacle of the separate nations of the West marching in parallel formation to a common drumbeat—a parade never visible in any previous period of extended social change, be it the fall of Rome, the rise of Christianity, or the advent of the Enlightenment. That determinism bestowed on society's "leftward" movement the aspect of a natural process. In an age that worshipped science it was understandable that such an interpretation was already tantamount to viewing social history as not only inevitable, but progressive.

A second reason for the progressive interpretation of history was that the institutional aspects of its dynamic embodied many specific characteristics by which the idea of progress was otherwise supposed to be manifested. The replacement of faith by rationality was one of these, insofar as capitalism was indisputably more rational than feudalism; and a central intellectual appeal of socialism was that it replaced the hidden irrationalities of capitalism with the presumed transparent rationality of a consciously planned society. Yet another widely accepted characteristic of progress was the extension of individual freedom, where again the leftward movement seemed entirely fitted to the aim. Capitalism had already discarded the narrow socio-political and economic constraints of vassalage and serfdom; socialism promised to end those of wage slavery, perhaps even of nationalism. And not least in this progressive interpretation of the economic transformation of society was its celebration of the central placement of human self-determination. Feudalism was generally agreed to be a society built on acceptance and resignation; capitalism was seen as a society of self-defining individuals; socialism as the first society consciously to take its very history into its own hands—the beginning of truly human history, as Engels put it.

There was, to be sure, always recognition that progress involved more than economics. As I have said, science was widely regarded as the very instantiation of progress, and applied science as its most clearcut manifestation. If science was not capitalism's natural child, applied science was assuredly its adopted child. The same claims could be made for the democratization of government, the attainment of social equality, and the general enlightenment of the citizenry. These too were easily seen as following in the wake of capitalism, with its rejection of ancient class differentials, its emphasis on liberty of contract and person, and its self-interest in the training and basic education of its population.

In the same vein, there has also been a tradition of opposition to a materialist view of progress, expressed in the visions of the Utopian socialists or in the Marxian rejection of the capitalist value system in its entirety. Even here, however, we find a persisting belief in the relevance, not to say centrality, of economics to the attainment of progress. Thus, whereas the arguments against capitalism centered on the ills that arose from its failings *as an economic system,* the arguments in favor of socialism also rested on the liberation and self-fulfillment that socialism would offer *as an economic system.* To put it differently, there is very little rhetoric of politics or culture in the literatures of anti-capitalism and pro-socialism. The discussion is conducted in the vocabulary of economics.

I trust it is by now clear that I do not start with the idea of a progressive economic interpretation of history as a straw man to be demolished before we turn to more serious matters. On the contrary, I seek to make clear why its hold on our conception of progress has been so powerful and persistent. Such a recognition is necessary, I think, to gain some perspective on the feelings of dismay that are so much part of our contemporary frame of mind. Certainly the axis that indicated progress in terms of a movement leftward has no relevance to the Russian shambles, where Left and Right seem to have changed places. What relevance does the concept have to the situation in Yugoslavia, Somalia, the Union of South Africa, Iran? Would not indices more appropriate to those parts of the world be better labelled Up and Down, or Forward and Back?

Of course this raises the question of what those other indices might measure. Morality? Politics? Whatever the answers, they are very unlikely to have the internal coherency and persuasiveness that are the peculiar attributes of economics as a mode of social observation and judgment. Smithian, Marxian, Keynesian, and Schum-

peterian views of history are not "wrong." Each calls to
our attention inner logics of change that might not otherwise have been observed, and each imbues those logics
with moral significance as well as "scientific" clarity. The
disconcerting aspect of the present situation lies precisely
in our inability to apply such an overarching interpretation to events. The behavior of the Serbian fighters and
the Somalian bandits, of the supporters of apartheid and
the fiery-eyed Islamic clergy, of resurgent fascist groups
in Europe and the religious Right in the United States all
lie outside the framework by which we have made
"sense" out of events. The terrible images they project
for us to see on television and read about in the newspapers seem to have no "rationale," no "explanation," no
"understandability"—which is to say, no place within
the scheme of history as we have learned to construe it.
As such, they bring home with unsettling force that there
exist other frameworks before which we stand not only
aghast, but uncomprehending.

These frameworks have been around long prior to the
very idea of progress, much less its denomination in
terms of economic processes. I think of the overriding
importance of kinship relations in establishing social
norms and relations; of the paranoid suspicion of ethnic
or cultural "others"; of the celebration of unreason and
the glorification of power. The "outrageous" behaviors
of our own time testify that these ancient frameworks
may have been pushed to one side, but they have not
been outgrown or discarded by the economic processes
we take for granted as both the driving and the binding
forces of society.

There is, finally, a still more sobering thought. Outrageous behaviors can be perceived all through history, including during the era in which the economic view of progress was itself coming into prominence. The sobering thought is that this economic view is likely to lose its cogency over the coming decades, certainly over the coming century. The problems of capitalism mount. As we have seen, their containment lies ever more in the care of political processes for which we have no reassuring frameworks of analytic clarity and progressive implication. Even the collapse of the Soviet system, everywhere hailed as a victory for human freedom, has not yet been fully assessed as the defeat it has been for human aspirations.

History's lesson therefore warns us that modern-day consciousness has been formed in a period that is now moving to a close. The confidence natural to a society sustained by belief in an impersonal momentum of progress is less likely to emerge in a society uncertain as to the availability of economic solutions, much less self-generated ones. A search for new understandings is sure to take their place, in which Up and Down and Foreward and Back displace Left and Right as the crucial axes of social movement. Alas, the punishment that history may visit upon us is that of discovering that there are no forces that promise to drive society in the new directions in which we seek to move.

II

Whatever forms Up and Down may take, it seems very likely that they will embody something connected with the idea of socialism. By "socialism" I mean a society unmistakably disconnected from the very idea of economic determinism. The disjointures may be of many kinds, but in the line of my argument, the most important kind must be a severance from capitalism's most powerful history-shaping characteristic—namely, its subordination of behavior to economic imperatives.

There are two reasons why economic-driven behavior cannot become the order-generating force for any society to which the socialist label could be properly attached. The first, often featured in critical literature, is that societies driven by the need to accumulate capital, and subjected to the pressures of the market, suffer from severe deformations, including the alienated consciousness induced by extensive commercialization, the deformation of individual character caused by the over-division of labor, and the socially harmful bias toward self-directed, rather than other-directed values. A second, less familiar but no less serious objection is that a general subordination of action to impersonal action-directives demotes progress itself from a consciously intended social aim to an unintended consequence of action, thereby robbing it of moral content. My specification for socialism thereby places it under the aegis of Up and Forward, rather than Left—an assignment that carries a strong moral message, but that is also an admission that we do not know what may be its internal dynamics.

Prior to considerations of morality must come those of feasibility—namely, whether a noncapitalist society is "possible." The question has two meanings. The first is whether such a society could assure the allocation of labor and the fit between inputs and outputs needed to assure sheer survivability. The question can easily be answered affirmatively insofar as socialist societies are imagined as change-avoiding, tradition-centered communities—the Kalahari Bush people in Western clothes. This may be a viable socialism, particularly if ecological disaster should ever hit, but it is not one we can seriously contemplate before such an event.

A more difficult problem concerns societies that entrust their coherence and continuity to central planning. The former Soviet Union is, of course, the arch-example here, and its collapse is widely regarded as a warning that such societies are bound to fail. I am not sure that charge can be levied with certainty. The collapse may well have been the consequence of bringing to bear on the problem of planning the worst traditions of a bureaucratic autocracy, a primitive technology of communication, and the extreme pressures of the Cold War. Had capitalism been initially launched under such conditions, it too might well have failed. Against prevailing opinion, then, I would think that the feasibility of a centrally planned socialism should be considered an open question, always assuming that such a society were not forced into continuous economic reorganization, whether from external or internal pressures.

This is not an altogether satisfactory answer because the prevailing conception of a desirable socialism does not usually include static societies, for cultural reasons, or centrally planned ones, for political reasons (they have no Switzerland). The question then turns to the possibility of creating a viable non-traditional, non-centralized, and non-market system. Recently Michael Albert and Robin Hahnel have suggested an intriguing solution to this problem.[54] I can only sketch in some of its novel features here. Their plan envisages a society organized to maximize the participatory rather than the antagonistic relation of its members. Its internal coherence would be achieved by a system of "voting" that would establish the overall shape of productive flows. The "socialist" aspect of the economic plan would reside more in the social constraints affecting voters' choices than in the planning process itself. A solidaristic ethos would be encouraged by obliging all members to undertake some work outside their principal tasks, on a regular basis. A noninvidious lifestyle would be encouraged by establishing norms of overall consumption applicable to all. The possibility of technological and organizational innovation would be encouraged, but also restrained by elaborate forms of review and voting for all such proposed changes.

Could such a social order work? To ourselves, socialized into a quite different mode of life, it seems hopelessly naive, utopian, against human nature. Yet, to most of the

---

54. See Michael Albert and Robin Hahnel, *Looking Forward: Participatory Economics for the Twenty-First Century,* Boston, South End Press, 1991, and *The Political Economy of Participatory Economics,* Princeton, N.J., Princeton University Press, 1991. The first is a popular introduction; the second a formal economic exposition.

humans who have ever lived on this earth, I suspect that our own lifeways would appear equally, perhaps even more, unnatural—I remind us of the consternation of the village elders to whom we tried to explain a market system. A participatory society would, of course, pose organizational problems. Its smooth functioning would require some market-like coordination mechanism. Like any other society, it would have to generate a regular supply of labor for unpleasant or routine work. It would need to restrain individuals from pursuing antisocial ends in their economic activities. Some of these problems would be resolved by the normal pressures of social conformity. Others would require new technologies, new institutions, and above all, a new conception of how the economic aspect of life would be integrated with social and political life. Inevitably, with new institutions will come new problems. I have given only the sketchiest outline of what such a participatory economy might be like, to indicate that it represents a genuinely novel, technically workable, and morally attractive arrangement for the future.

Do I therefore think it will be the direction of things during the twenty-first century? I do not. The transition is too difficult; the rearrangements too complex; and above all, the opposition too ferocious for any such revolutionary change to occur in so short a time, historically speaking. Participatory economics will not become the social order in the twenty-first century, no matter what, catastrophes included.

Nevertheless, ideas have a life of their own. It is not impossible that the goals and the general social conception of a participatory order might enter our consciousness over the coming century. I should think that its ideas and ideals would serve us in good purpose while we wrestle with the huge problems of making capitalism work as well as possible as long as possible. During these years, when tensions and failures are more likely to be the order of the day than resolutions and successes, it will help to have another social destination in our imaginations.

Is it then still possible to believe in socialism as a realistic and welcome destination during the coming long decades? As I have said, it is certainly possible that advanced and adaptive capitalisms—what I have elsewhere called "slightly imaginary Swedens"—will make their appearance. However humane and farsighted, these are still societies within the force field of capitalism, driven by the need to accumulate capital, coordinated by a market mechanism. Two problems make it difficult to foresee movement beyond the borders of such advanced systems. The first is the resistance that it would encounter. Albert and Hahnel say nothing with regard to the opposition that their proposal would be certain to adduce among the upper and upper-middle classes whose favored position would be undermined by it.

And even that is not quite an end to the problem. The real question, it seems to me, is what concept will replace that of progress in a postcapitalist society. Perhaps the answer is that there will be none, and that an achieved socialism will simply be the sum of many individual lives pursued within a benign social setting. As I have said, looking back over the long past, we find no concept of progress before the advent of capitalism. In its place

there have been stoicism and resignation, the great ano-
dynes of humanity, and visions of an afterlife, its great
consolatory fantasy. These might become the regnant
ideas of socialism, but they do not accord with our present views of what socialism should be. In my judgment,
at least, progress measured along some axis of Up and
Forward remains Socialism's guiding idea, not resignation or religiosity.

Need I add that we know next to nothing of the dynamics of Up and Forward, having put aside their realization through "economic" motivations? Perhaps that is
only to say that the character of postcapitalist civilization
must depend on the motivations to which its citizens
would respond, the constraints they would accept, the
goals they would establish. That does not tell us whether
or not such societies may come into existence. Like much
else in history that remains unknowable. It does, however, make of the idea of socialism either an inspiring or a
frightening prospect, largely depending on what we perceive to be the characteristics of human nature itself.

III

I propose to introduce the treacherous idea of human
nature by quoting David Hume. "Would you know the
sentiments, inclinations and course of life of the Greeks
and Romans?" he asked in his *Enquiry Concerning
Human Understanding*. "Study well the temper and actions of the French and English. . . . Mankind are so
much the same, in all times and places, that history in-

forms us of nothing new or strange in this particular."[55]

Thus, human nature was to Hume a great Rosetta stone by which to decipher the actions of men distant or near, ancient or (in all likelihood) future. But this emphasis on a transcultural unity is not all that Hume implies. Continuing his thought, he writes: "Should a traveller, returning from a far country, bring us an account of men . . . who were entirely divested of avarice, ambition, or revenge, who knew no pleasure but friendship, generosity, and public spirit; we should immediately . . . prove him a liar, with the same certainty as if he stuffed his narration with stories of centaurs and dragons, miracles and prodigies."

Hume thus believes that it is impossible to imagine a future that will depart from the general tenor of the past. I need hardly add that this view can be hardened into an ironclad version of history's lessons. Nonetheless, let us suppose that Hume's traveller returned today from America in 2070. Would we ourselves not greet his report with Hume's skepticism? Does this not imply that any vision of progress that abandons the narrow boundaries of economism and aspires to a higher plane is a chimera, and that socialism is therefore, at its best, no more than a means to a more effective, perhaps even more humane mode of organizing the labors of society, but not for its moral elevation?

Let me present a second argument for Hume's skepticism: Here is a vision of the personality that can be expected to appear once the pressures and deformations of

55. David Hume, *An Enquiry Concerning Human Understanding*, Chicago, Open Court, 1935, pp. 85–86.

existing society are removed, and liberated man steps forth. What exactly is to be expected of such a man, asks one strong supporter of the concept—whether sincerely or tongue in cheek is hard to say:

One might say [she writes] that the liberated man is the generous and disinterested man; he is also a creative man, who can express his personality and talents in creative action without constraint, whether in manual, intellectual, or artistic work, or in his relations to other men. . . . He is an individual without idols, dogmas, prejudices or a priori ideas. He is tolerant, inspired by a profound sense of justice and equality, and aware of himself as being at the same time an *individual* and a *universal* man.[56]

Why is this expression of hope so implausible? The answer must spring from the same referential base that forces us to admit the cogency of Hume's case. It is an appeal to a set of half clearcut, half inarticulated concepts by which we establish a "nature" of man that tells us, however imperfectly, what we can expect of others and what we cannot.

Can we formulate such a concept of human nature with all its evident risks? I think its core can be succinctly expressed: the adult personality emerges only after its possessor has run the gamut of infantile dependency. All advanced species gain some portion of their "natures" from similar periods of infantile conditioning, but in no species is the dependency so protracted and therefore so crucially important as it is with humans. I would call this

56. Mathilde Niel, "The Phenomenon of Technology," in Erich Fromm, *Socialist Humanism,* Garden City, N.Y., Doubleday, 1965, p. 306.

a psychoanalytically informed view of human nature.

Such a view enters into our expectations regarding human behavior by its insistence—along with Marx—that "men make their own history, but they do not make it just as they please."[57] For Marx the constraints on behavior are those of social relations; for Freud and his successors it is those of their infantile relations. This by no means closes off possibilities for social change any more than did Marx's incubus of the past rule out revolutionary action in the future. It only establishes that the protagonists in history, without exception, will have run the gantlet and experienced its blows. Empathic parenting and supportive institutions can undoubtedly instill many social routines other than our own, but they cannot produce "liberated" behavior—that is, behavior free of sublimated rage, denials of many kinds, and actings-out of fantasies of oppression, both in an active as well as a passive mode. These infantile yearnings are never overcome, only expressed in many disguises. They linger in us all to form a substratum of what we call human nature—a substratum whence arises the susceptibility to much "irrational" action, including that of the political and social behavior that today imbue so much of current history with a sense of incomprehensibility.

In this disquieting situation, the sober, even somber prospects for material improvement in the most sheltered and advantaged capitalisms—never mind the horrendous outlook for some entire continents and subcontinents—exacerbates the prevailing anxiety. The eco-

---

57. Emile Burns, ed., *A Handbook of Marxism,* New York, Random House, 1935, "The Eighteenth Brumaire of Louis Bonaparte", p. 116.

nomic, technological, and ecological challenges of our time seem likely to lessen the mobilizing capability of capitalism, increasing the susceptibility of our unconscious energies to more ancient appeals of ethnic tribalisms, religious frenzies, and other such sublimations. Thus as the dynamic of "leftward" progress weakens, that conjured up by the social labels of Up and Down, Forward and Backward increases, but by no means in directions along those axes that we would wish.

What does this portend for twenty-first century capitalism? It is a question that can be better answered with respect to the social formation as a whole than for any individual entity within it. We know, in general, the problems against which capitalism must contend, and the motivations and structures that will establish the terms of its encounter with them. Capitalism is assuredly a social order that draws its acquisitive energies from the unconscious substratum of behavior, and it must therefore expect to evidence both the energy and the irrationality of that motivating drive. It is structured in a manner that forces choices between the public and the private realms, but the social order typically misrepresents both sides, underplaying the negative aspects of the private realm, overplaying those of the public realm. Hence, the allocation of tasks between the political and economic sectors is often seriously wrong. Not least, capitalism entrusts its overall economic coordination to a mechanism that is clearly inadequate to resolve the most pressing problems of our coming century—namely, the internationalization of production and the globalization of our ecological encounter. One cannot contemplate this catalogue of deficiencies and expect the order as a whole to make the passage through the twenty-first century unscathed. No social order structured as ours is can make that passage without far-reaching changes in its institutions.

At the same time, an overview of capitalism's nearer-term prospects suggests another general estimation of its outlook. Although its underlying drives stem from the irrational depths of the psyche, the channels through which capitalism directs those energies have provided an agency of unparalleled effectiveness for advancing material betterment. Under different institutional guidance, that material advancement can probably continue for some generations, albeit under worsening circumstances and against more daunting problems. So, too, although the market mechanism is responsible for mammoth misdirections of effort, it has also performed prodigies of social coordination. That general capability still seems usable for a considerable period, if its domain of authority is suitably narrowed. In much the same manner, the dual realms of capitalism seem as well qualified as any institutional—not merely constitutional—arrangement to protect individual liberty in the next stage of capitalism, as in the last. Finally, and perhaps of greatest importance in the short run, no alternative social order seems within grasp, at least in the century that serves as a metaphor for the reach of our imagination.

Therefore, wars and disasters aside, and even in the face of the global warming that will likely become the central challenge of the coming century, capitalism bids fair to remain the dominant social order during our children's and children's children's time. But that is not quite an end to it. The partial remissions of its long-term sentence apply with special significance to those of us who live in its favored enclaves, and who can therefore best take advantage of the range of behaviors compatible with the requirements of the social order. If, as seems likely, there is a threshold of necessary acquisitiveness to maintain the system's *élan vital,* so there is also a limit beyond which acquisitiveness no longer serves, and may well disserve, the adaptability of the order. In the same way, if there is a threshold of necessary economic indifference to allow the market to function properly—a willingness to allow individuals to take their chances in the contest for economic places—there is also a limit beyond which indifference turns into a dysfunctional social injustice. So, too, if the recognition of a separate economic realm provides capitalism with its unique protection against an all-pervasive political authority, it is all too easy to conclude that the ultimate strength of a people lies in the achievement of economic and not political goals. There is, in other words, a distance between the behaviors and attitudes that a capitalist society requires, and those that it tolerates or encourages at its own peril. On each nation's self-determined placement between these behaviors and attitudes will depend its chances for adaptation to the demands of the coming century.

Thus I come again to the only prediction I have allowed myself to make, and that I must now iterate one last time. The twenty-first century capitalism will be dominated by a spectrum of capitalisms, some successful, some not. The crucial question for Americans, and perhaps for the world as a whole, is where our own nation will be located along that spectrum. I have previously spoken of "slightly imaginary Sweden" as one end of a range of capitalist societies. I now add that it is equally possible to speak of not-so-imaginary America as another. In the context of twentieth-century realities, Sweden proved to be unworkable. In the context of twenty-first century realities, America may prove to be the same, unless it changes mightily.

A last word seems necessary. I am not so foolhardy as to believe that a framework of uncertain analysis and personal vision will enable us to circumvent Kliuchevsky's admonition. Perhaps history's punishments are its lessons. Nonetheless, it is my hope that some grasp of what the twenty-first century holds in store for capitalism may enable us to avoid at least some of the punishments we will otherwise have to endure.

Index